Studies in Intellectual History

Studies

in

Intellectual

History

BOAS
CHERNISS
CHINARD
EDELSTEIN
GLASS
SPITZER
STIMSON
TEMKIN
WIENER

GREENWOOD PRESS, PUBLISHERS
NEW YORK   1968

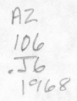

ARTHUR ONCKEN LOVEJOY

SOCII SOCIO
MAGISTRO DISCIPULI
AMICI AMICO

Table of Contents

Table of Contents

Studies in Intellectual History

GEORGE BOAS

Some Problems of Intellectual History

The following remarks are made in order to bring together in one place a statement of the various problems which confront the historian of ideas from time to time. I cannot claim to have answered all the questions nor to have stated all the problems involved, but as far as one man's experience goes, these are the most frequent.

I. The first problem one has to face squarely is the problem of just what an idea is. By last count the word itself had some forty-two distinct meanings. I shall spare you the list since no one could keep it straight anyway. What I mean by an idea is something which might be asserted in a declarative statement, an assertion of belief, the solution of a problem, not necessarily one's own problem, but someone's in the last analysis. Such assertions may be statements of fact or of policy, as is obvious, and sometimes though phrased as statements of fact they may conceal statements of policy. Their truth and falsity, again obviously, do not concern the historian of ideas, but their precise meaning does.

(1) Now at this point one finds that a misconception frequently occurs. Historians of ideas are asked whether they are not engaged in what used to be called semasiology, the history of the meaning of words. That misconception can be eliminated perhaps by pointing out the following facts: (a) sometimes the

same idea is named by a variety of words. The most dramatic
cases of this which occur to me are the cases of the idea of an
object and the idea of egoism. If one reads seventeenth and eighteenth century books in philosophy, one will come across the
words, "subjective" and "egoism." In the twentieth century these
words indicate, respectively, something occurring in the mind as
distinguished from something occurring in the material and
external worlds, and a doctrine of morals which implies a kind
of selfishness. But at the time when we first find them, the word
"subjective" meant something existing in the external world,
in the substratum, a descendant of Aristotle's *hypokeimenon*, and
the word "egoism" meant what we call "solipsism." Now the
ideas that there is an external world and that only the self exists
did not change much, though theories of what the characteristics
of both were have changed a good deal. Hence if one substitutes
the ideas for the words and semasiology for the history of ideas,
one is clearly confused. (b) Sometimes, as Mr. Lovejoy has so
successfully pointed out on many occasions, the same word is
used for a great variety of ideas. His classic article on the discrimination of romanticisms is a case in point, and to that we
might add his appendix to our volume, *Primitivism in Antiquity*, in which he discriminated sixty-six meanings of the
word "nature" and its derivatives. But we need not go to the
historians for evidence of this. One has only to think of the
ambiguities in the words "democracy," "progress," "Chris-
tianity," and "poetry" in contemporary discussions to see that
one can never be sure that a given word is the label for a single
idea.

(2) Analogous to this confusion between a word and an idea,
one must point out an error which frequently is made to the
effect that if a word is found, like "romanticism" or "Chris-
tianity" or "poetry," the things it names must of necessity cover

a common meaning and that all one has to do is to collect all the things named by it and by abstraction find the common meaning, a hidden essence remaining self-identical through time and under the layers of ambiguities. I am far from sure of why this error occurs and one would imagine that at least those people who have ever come in contact with undergraduates would understand how words change their meanings sometimes to a ludicrous extent. When one receives an undergraduate report in which the word " meretricious " is confused with " meritorious " and the word " nugatory " with " highly important," one does not usually conclude there must be a common meaning in each pair of words but rather writes a sneering comment in the margin. If, however, the undergraduates were long dead and their papers were in print and one were following the technique which I am deprecating, one would be forced to that conclusion. The proper conclusion to be made is that the words in question are ambiguous and hence stand for two or more different ideas.

Thus to take a more serious example, the fact that *Hamlet* is called a tragedy and that *The Trojan Woman* is called a tragedy does not in itself imply anything whatsoever about there being a tragic essence common to them both, though in actual fact there may be one. Similarly after the discrimination of the romanticisms made by Lovejoy, there ought to be no further discussion of what romanticism *really* was. There happen to have been a variety of aesthetic doctrines, some of which were logically related to others and some of which were not, all called by the same name. But that fact does not imply they all had a common essence any more than the fact that hundreds of people are called John Smith means that they are all of the same parentage. This is perhaps the most common and most misleading error arising from the confusion of ideas and words. One could speak for hours about it alone and perhaps should.

It should be observed that I am not maintaining that all names for ideas are ambiguous nor that the reasons for the ambiguity cannot be discovered.

II. We have said that an idea, as we use the term, is an assertion, a statement of fact or of policy, and that sometimes the two are intertwined in the mind of the person who holds the idea. Thus in Poe's lecture, *The Poetic Principle*, one finds the statement, " I hold that a long poem does not exist." It is clear to most people that the *Iliad* is both long and a poem and an existent poem. But it appears at once that Poe means by the word *poem* something both eulogistic and descriptive. A real poem, as distinguished from an ostensible poem to his way of thinking is a set of verses which " elevate the soul." Just what this elevation or, as he also calls it, excitement is, he never makes quite clear, but that is of small moment here. What is of moment is the actual fact that Poe for some reason or other did not use the word " poem " for poems which he disliked or of which he disapproved, as some congressmen prefer to call Americans with whose ideas they disagree un-American. Thus the normative meaning of a term is confused with the descriptive meaning. We find this confusion particularly noticeable in the fields of aesthetics and ethics and politics and religion, in other words wherever man's love and hate and fear and aspirations are concerned.

But it must also be noticed that such confusion is not peculiar to the field of ideas. The names we use to classify a variety of things are useful only in so far as things actually possess the traits implied in the generic terms. But there will always be a certain fringe of difference between what the generic term demands and what the instances exhibit. According to Aristotle this difference always was to be found in what he called the accidental, rather than the essential, traits. But the great question was that of determining what was essence and what accident. The distinction was easier for Aristotle than for us, because he believed in an order of Nature as opposed to a world of chance in the former of which there was no matter, a belief obscured in most historians of philosophy but nevertheless very important for an understanding of Aristotle. Accidental traits appeared in the latter of these two realms.

By analogy, Poe seems to have believed that there was a poetic essence which was perceived by what he called the " Poetic Sentiment," which he also calls " Taste," one of the three faculties of the soul, of which the other two were the " Reason " and the " Moral Sense." Hence, as for Aristotle a biologist might be mistaken in identifying a certain animal or plant, so for Poe a critic might be mistaken in spotting a poem. It is strange that he did not raise the question how or why people used their reason or moral sense to discern the object of taste. We usually do not try to discriminate colors with our ears or notes with our tongues. But we must not be led astray by irrelevant if interesting problems. What the historians of ideas might profitably discuss in this context is the idea that there exists such a faculty as taste with the properties which Poe believed to inhere in it. But all that I am attempting to do here is to indicate how a program which seems at first sight to be purely descriptive contains within it a normative element of such power that its author should in all fairness assert not that he is, for instance, writing an account of what poetry is but of what it ought to be.

The idea in a case like this must be broken down into its two component parts. Part of the idea is the superiority of one kind of poetry to another. The second part is the theory that human beings possess a certain faculty called " Taste " which perceives the kind of beauty which Poe was particularly interested in. It is clear that each component part could be defended or attacked separately, that the truth of one does not depend upon the truth of the other, that consequently a person might believe in one without believing in the other, and that therefore two ideas are involved here rather than one. One can state this differently by maintaining that Poe's idea of poetry was a complex which could only be expressed in two logically independent statements.

One type of critic of the history of ideas will assert at this point that Poe was not aware of all this and for all I know he would be right. The historian of ideas is not merely occupied with what proponents of an idea are aware of, though this of course interests him too, but also with what is involved in the idea by logic. This brings us to the third main point.

III. Mr. Philip Merlan recently published in the *Journal of the History of Ideas* a short article on Lucretius, the burden of which was that Lucretius was neither a primitivist nor a believer in progress. If a primitivist be defined as a man believing that man as he first appeared on earth or man in a state of nature—let us leave the definition of that state alone in this place—and if a believer in progress be defined as a man who believes that human conditions of life are better than they used to be, it is true that one can also believe in a doctrine that man's life is neither better nor worse than it used to be or that civilized life is no better nor worse than uncivilized. That was not Mr. Merlan's thesis. On the contrary, his reason was to the effect that Lucretius was neither primitivistic nor antiprimitivistic, " because it does not seem that he wanted to treat the problem at all." [1] Let us assume that Lucretius did not want to treat the problem. It is nevertheless true that there appears in *De Rerum Natura* an account of history which is antiprimitivistic. This account was read by many people and influenced their thinking and indeed may possibly have changed their minds. Similarly Poe's theory of

[1] *Journal of the History of Ideas*, Vol. XI, 368.

poetry was presumably derived from his reading of Coleridge and Coleridge derived his from his reading of certain German philosophers. If we give to that theory a name ending in *ism*, then the German *ism* reappears in Poe whether Poe knew it or not, whether he would have liked to be known as a follower of the German philosophers or not, whether he would have given the same reasons for it as they gave or not, and so on. As for Lucretius, we do not know precisely where he found his account of history, though we can guess that he found it in writings of the Epicurean school if not in those of its founder. It would be of course of great interest to know whether Lucretius really believed in his account of progress or not, but that is irrelevant to the question of whether the passage in question is primitivistic or not. One has only to read it to see. One need know nothing of its author's intentions.

Most of the listeners to *Fidelio* and Wagner's *Ring* know little of the political background of those operas, nor was their influence on subsequent history attributable to the political ideas involved in them. As far as Wagner was concerned, he rejected them in later life. But this does not mean that these ideas were not there. Hence it is important to remember that an author's sincerity has nothing to do with the meaning of what he says and the historian of ideas must catch them where they occur. If Mr. Merlan is right, then we have an idea appearing in an author who did not believe in it; if I am right in thinking that most people do not see the politics in *Fidelio* and the *Ring*, then we have an idea which becomes ineffectual, perhaps because expressed in a medium which obscured its meaning. Most of us know, I take it, that Spenser's *Faery Queene* was an allegory, but there must be dozens of people who have read it, as I did for the first time, without any notion at all that it was anything more than a series of knightly adventures. Historians of ideas are interested in an author's intentions in so far as the meaning of his ideas is concerned; but they are not necessarily interested in his other intentions. When a man is so ironical that his irony disappears, what he has to say obviously will be interpreted as if it were not irony.

IV. The reason for dwelling on this point is that ideas have a way of occurring in places where one would least expect them. Mr. Malcolm Cowley has written an article in the New York *Herald-Tribune* [2] in which he made out a good case for the thesis that *The Scarlet Letter* was planned in five major episodes or acts analogous to those of a Greek tragedy. This technique, he says, was expounded by Poe some time earlier in his review of *Twice Told Tales*. Let us assume for the sake of simplicity that Mr. Cowley is right. It would be an interesting problem to discover how Hawthorne got this idea which was to appear in *Mme Bovary* and in some of the novels of Henry James and which gives them what we call their unity of action. Now that Hawthorne did apply this tragic outline for his novel is, let us say, established as a fact. But novels had been written for many generations with no novelist thinking of using it. On what basis could one have predicted that the technique would have been used in a novel written by a New England author who had so far composed, as far as most people knew, no novels? Looking backwards, it is easy enough to see that he did apply it and why a man desirous of unity should have applied it. But one has only to think of the novels which had been written before 1850 to see how original the method was. One might argue that the very nature of a novel is such that one need make no sacrifices to such unity, providing as it does the means of introducing picturesque episodes, minor characters of all sorts, comic relief, the kind of

[2] August 6, 1950.

10

mechanical balance which one finds so often in Thackeray, the vast scenes which Dickens was fond of, and so on.

But whether one is writing a novel or a play, one is still telling a story, and that the Greek tragedy should inspire the outline of a novel may not strike my readers as forcibly as it strikes me. Let me give another example. The idea that the cosmos is a balance of determinism and freedom, of mechanism and spontaneity, is a metaphysical idea whose roots go back at least as far as Leibniz but which appeared in full flower in Schelling. But this idea also appears in another form in the aesthetic writings of the Schlegels. It occurs also in the preface to *Cromwell* and from then on seems to be a common feature of many so-called romantic novels. But aesthetically, the determined and the free appear as the sublime and the absurd. Polarization of this sort then pops up in literary criticism and we find Shakespeare praised for what Voltaire disliked so heartily in him, the disunity which is "expressed," as the Schlegels would have said, in the union of the grotesque and the serious. There is no comic relief in Greek tragedy unless as a colleague of mine once suggested, it occurs in the choruses; nor is there any in Seneca nor the French classic dramatists. I do not pretend to know why Shakespeare and his predecessors and successors went in for comic relief, but I am pretty certain that it was not for the reasons which Hugo gave.[3] Nor do I see any reason whatsoever why dramas or novels or any other works of art should attempt to mirror the structure of the universe. Who could have predicted on logical grounds that a metaphysical theory would turn into an aesthetic program?

I shall give but a third example in order to save space and time. Miss Nicolson has already illustrated how science invaded the field of poetry after Newton, and indeed before. And we all

[3] But see Ola E. Winslow's *Low Comedy as a Structural Element in English Drama* (Chicago, 1926), 122 ff.

know how biology invaded the field of novel-writing in Zola. I should like to indicate how science has invaded the field of painting. Mr. Alexander Dorner in his eloquent book on Herbert Bayer, *The Way beyond "Art,"* points out that Bayer's paintings can only be appreciated if one sees in them objects in space-time, not spatial objects outside of time. Because of that one sees planes in interpenetration, with an emphasis upon the dynamic aspects of lines. It is clear that the world we see with our eyes is not that in which material objects interpenetrate. Try as we will we cannot see them thus, any more than we can walk through solid walls, whatever energy may be able to do. Hence it still appears strange to us to see the world as Bayer depicts it.

Moreover, there is no reason why a painter should feel obligated to represent matter according to physics, rather than according to eyesight. He is of course free to do anything he wishes, and I do not deny that Bayer's paintings and drawings are a great deal more interesting and emotionally powerful than those of Alma-Tadema. But at the same time it must be granted that there exists no legislature to decree that a painter must desert the macroscopic world of vision for the microscopic world of mathematical physics. The apology for the latter will be probably that the painter is occupied with representing " reality " and " reality " will be defined as the subject matter of the physical sciences. That is pure nonsense if the unreal is defined as the realm of illusions, ghosts, hallucinations, and their like. In other words, a scientific idea has appeared in aesthetics though it has no logical relation to aesthetics, except that established by fiat. Let me repeat that what I say is not said in depreciation of Mr. Dorner or Bayer.

What this amounts to is the caution that the absence of a logical tie between an idea and its application or reinterpretation is no evidence of its absence. Metaphysical ideas may turn up in educational policy; political ideas may turn up in music; astronomical ideas may turn up in aesthetic theory. This, I might add, is one of those things which makes the history of ideas so highly interesting, for it illustrates the play of the human imagination in a field usually thought to be essentially foreign to imagination.

V. But none of this is intended to suggest that the historian of ideas should indulge in what Lovejoy has called mind reading. We are writing history, not psychology, and if a man is inconsistent, that fact must be noted. There is no law compelling a man to be logical and indeed one of the most noticeable facts about intellectual exercises is that the discipline of logic breaks down so frequently. Even the most famous thinkers can be shown to have been unaware of the conflicts in their thoughts. Hence it is against the rules to insist that a man must have been logically sound and that contradictions in his ideas can and must be explained away. We have a tendency to imagine that every writer has a system of philosophy into which he has succeeded in incorporating all his thoughts. Even in those cases where systematic reasoning is most pronounced, as in the case of Aristotle, there are conflicts which cannot be resolved. It would thus be self-defeating to try to discover an underlying unity in him. I do not maintain that the thinkers in question knew that they were inconsistent or that they wanted to be inconsistent. But they are frequently blind to their inconsistencies and the point at which they swerve from the path of logical exactitude is a point of the greatest interest to the historians.

Now there are two cases in contemporary historical research where another kind of mind reading is usually found. (a) In Marxist interpretation of ideological history the historian is forced to maintain that the thinker, whether he knew it or not, is really expressing the ideas of the dominant social class or the class with which he has, often unconsciously, identified himself. Thus Newton's astrophysics turns out to have been written for the English navigators and *Uncle Tom's Cabin* for the cotton-mill owners of Lowell and Lawrence and Fall River. Much clever and doubtless valid work has been done in the field of the economic interpretation of history, but before one can make the correlation between a set of ideas and an economic complex, it would be necessary to know more than we do know about the aetiology of thought. Of that more later.

(b) A close associate of the Marxist is the psychoanalyst. He too has to indulge in mind reading, for he too believes that ideas are always rationalizations. The meaning of an idea for him too is something below the level of consciousness and he presumably knows how to reach that level. I have not the competence to say how valid the psychoanalytic technique is, but anyone can observe for himself that if a given idea can be proved to be either the expression of the Oedipus complex, or of the inferiority complex, or of the collective unconscious with equal force, then there is no general agreement about what it precisely is. Here again I recognize the extremely important therapeutic work of psychoanalysis and would not for a moment join those who either sneer at it or denounce it. But we are talking about a field in which its relevance has not been demonstrated. In fact, one of the results of our work might be to provide the psychoanalyst with material for his study, for before he can draw any conclusions about the relations between the unconscious and the ratiocinative processes, he must know in detail just what thoughts are present.

In other words, ideas are the beliefs of people, what they assert. They are not, as we use the term, what they would have asserted had they known what we know, or what they should have asserted had they been consistent, or what they might have asserted had they drawn the conclusions from their premises which we would draw. So much is a matter of historiography or, if one wish, psychology, but there is also a logical fallacy which is sometimes committed by historians of ideas. It consists in arguing back from a conclusion to a supposedly necessary premise. This obviously is the fallacy of affirming the consequent of a hypothetical syllogism. For instance, an historian might argue that if a man pleaded for the rule of force, that the weaker must go to the wall and that insane asylums, hospitals, education, protection of the weak, and so on should be done away with, he must also be a Darwinian in his biological views. But that clearly is not so. For as all students of elementary logic know, a given conclusion may follow from a variety of premises.

VI. We come now to a question which is still a matter of dispute but upon which an historian must take a stand. That is the question both of the efficacy and aetiology of ideas. The two popular theories of Marxism and psychoanalysis both agree in denying that ideas as such have any efficacy to speak of—the qualification is necessary in both cases—and that the causes lie below the threshold of consciousness or else in the material world. The historian of ideas, while he need not overlook the nonideal and nonconscious causes and effects, for that matter, of ideas is confined to the realm of asserted beliefs and his problem must in the very nature of study be confined to that field. His universe of discourse is bounded by what men are aware of asserting, though they may not be aware of why they assert what they do assert. It is no refutation of their findings to maintain that they have not told the whole story; no one ever has or could tell the whole story about anything.

There is, for instance, a famous passage in the *Origin of Species* in which Darwin correlates the amount of honey produced in a region with the number of spinsters living there, by pointing out that the greatest enemy of the honey bee is the field mouse, the greatest enemy of the field mouse the domestic cat, and the greatest protector of the domestic cat we might add the spinster. But one has yet to find an entomologist who would feel that he must include a study of celibacy in his studies of honey bees, though he perhaps ought to do so to tell the whole story. The historian of ideas might very well feel that he was presenting to the psychologist and to the economic historian materials for further investigation, neither asserting nor denying the relation of ideas to anything else in the universe.

But within the field of consciously asserted belief, there are questions which the historian cannot overlook. Is it true, for instance, that all ideas are linked logically, and that what is usually called influence can be traced exclusively through logical relations? This does not seem to be so even in the field of philosophy where logical deductions are so heavily accentuated. There are cases where a man's pupils or successors seem to have perceived in his writings and to have drawn out of them implications which he himself did not perceive. But there are two sets of beliefs which could not be derived in this way. They include the choice of premises and the perception of problems. The choice of premises, we know, is logically unmotivated, by which I mean that they cannot by their nature be logically demonstrated. That is why they are called premises. This is so old a story that there is no need of dwelling upon it here. But the perception of a problem is somewhat different and has not received the notices which it deserves. Almost all thinkers have noted exceptions to the rules which they have elaborated but have had a tendency to explain them away. As we have said, even Aristotle realized that the world below the moon was full of eccentricities. Things were not as they should be. But he explained such deviations from the norm as due to the presence of matter. A new scientific theory often arises when a man refuses to explain away such deviations from the norm and looks for a more general formula which will include them. It will be observed that the drive towards greater and greater generalization in science accompanies, as indeed it must, a similar development in language. And one of the causes of new ideas must surely be the possession of abstract terms in which to express the higher degree of abstraction which increasing generalization demands.

In the field of literature, as in all the arts, this factor in intellectual history has caused no end of trouble. For here we are in a field where human invention plays its part and the student is not simply perceiving exceptions to the rules, but these exceptions are being created by writers and other artists. Thus we start, so to speak, with a vocabulary developed by certain Greek and Roman writers to describe, let us say, the literature which they were acquainted with, a very limited literature indeed. That vocabulary having been fixed and made common to all scholars is used to describe literary works made by people who were neither Greeks nor Romans. Moreover, these people, innocent of the demand to be faithful to antiquity, have invented styles of writing and composition which the ancient terminology does not adequately describe. Yet it seems to be presupposed that it must adequately describe them. Hence the drive is towards the unification of all literatures and the discovery of an essence common to them all and identical with that found in the most ancient of them. To put the matter more simply, Shakespeare's plays are not called tragedies or comedies in order to show that they conformed to the prescriptions of Aristotle, but got these names simply from historical sources, and though ingenious work has been done by literary critics and aestheticians to demonstrate a common essence in all tragedies and comedies, the results have been sound only to the extent that the critics and aestheticians have eliminated from their subject matters precisely those details which located them in their historical setting. But the historian who abandons the world of time for that of eternity is turning his back on history and his face towards science—either sociology, psychology, metaphysics, or what you will. One could conceivably show what *Hamlet* has in common with Sophocles's *Antigone*—or for that matter with *Mourning becomes Electra*—and I do not deny that such studies might have their interest. But if one wants to study *Hamlet*, one must recognize its place in the space-time order.

Hamlet is not an idea but a play. And no idea is so completely particularized. For even if I should think, which I don't, that George Washington was dominated by the desire to make money speculating in federal lands, an idea which is pretty specific and which need not apply to any revolutionary hero other than Washington, yet since Washington left no document confessing his motives, we should have to demonstrate our point by more general ideas of which Washington was an example. But most ideas of which we study the history do have a date and a certain peculiar relevance to a place. Their meaning is colored by their historical setting. I should think this to be true of Plato's ideas about politics and Aristotle's about poetry, to take but two examples. The extent to which they were talking to us of whom they could have known nothing, is certainly very limited except in one of those metaphysical senses which drive some philosophers to desperation. We shall not elaborate this point now, but the peculiar thing about ideas is that though they do arise within a definite historical setting, they seem to have relevance to points beyond their setting. This is the anomaly of knowledge of which Lovejoy has made so much. The relevance, however, never goes into the future except by accident. It extends well beyond the thinker in space and into the past and indeed he thinks frequently that he is a prophet too. But it is precisely because he cannot foretell the amazing things which are going to happen to upset all his generalizations that his prophecies are so bad. To illustrate this with a concrete example, if Plato thought of a state as a city-state with only a few thousand inhabitants, what he had to say about politics can apply to a state occupying millions of square miles and inhabited by millions of people only by so great a loss of particularity that it loses all sense. He was to be sure talking about men, women, and children, and one can make a fine show of his universality. But it is not mankind which interests the historian; it is men, and that means that the differences between people are more important than their similarities.

This is particularly important for the historian of ideas, for one of his problems is precisely that of why a given thought takes on new meaning as time moves on. If a given idea were eternal, it would have no history. The Pythagorean theorem cannot be said to have had a history except in the sense that it was discovered at a given date by someone and was perhaps used in a variety of ways after its discovery. But the idea that mankind is a debased and miserable creature, conceived in sin and doomed to damnation, was not only discovered at a certain date by someone, but acquired new relevance as western European history went on. For the idea of what was sin changed, and so did the idea of who was responsible and who not, and so did the notion of responsibility, and hence the notion of punishment and its kinds and degrees, and hence the question of obedience to law both human and divine, and so on. Such is its situation in the historical sequence, and its logical relations to other ideas are but a small part of what the historian must consider. The Greeks, in spite of the myth of Prometheus, never developed, as far as I know, any theory of infant damnation. Yet logically it could have been inferred from the Titan's creation of man out of-clay, since the Prometheus legend includes the jealousy of Zeus, and the punishment for the bestowing of fire on mankind. But no Greek who has survived left us any doctrine of human depravity, though there are doctrines of human degeneration, and all forms of chronological primitivism involve something analogous to the Fall.

It must be at least tentatively concluded that we actually do not have a satisfactory explanation of the cause and effects of ideas. But we can trace their rise and spread and their mutations in some detail. We cannot then say either that no man draws the logical consequences out of the ideas of his predecessors nor that all men do. In the history of science it is pretty well recognized that the initiation of hypotheses is still an unknown and that something vaguely called the creative imagination has to be called upon to explain it. It is, of course, no explanation at all. It is likely that the same applies to the formation of all ideas. But that to be sure leaves us in no worse plight than that in which any other kind of historian finds himself when he is dealing with particulars. For no individual event or thing is explicable except in so far as it is a fair sample of a class. The historian would like to win the prestige which accrues to the scientist these days and therefore would like to have general laws, no matter how empty of content in terms of which he might phrase his data and his conclusions. But I am maintaining that though it would be absurd to assert dogmatically the impossibility of constructing a sociology or anthropology on the analogy of physical science, such a discipline would be quite different from history, as I am using the term here. It would be as different as biography is from psychobiology, or portraiture from physiognomonics. The banal French saying that there are no sicknesses, there are only sick people, is an illustration of the same point. When one is dealing with particulars one will always find a gap between the law and its exemplification. Just as every man has his own way of catching cold, so every nation has its own way of making war, and every philosopher his own way of handling an idea. If the question be raised why we call the diseases colds, and the disturbances war, and the ideas by an equally abstract name, the answer is that if we are going to talk about things at all, we have to use common nouns and adjectives.

VII. *Conclusion.* What I have tried to do in this paper is to point out some of the peculiarities of historiography and to indicate some of its problems in so far as they pertain to the history of ideas. Many of these things have been already adequately treated by Lovejoy whose essays in this field and whose book, *The Great Chain of Being*, have established a model for such research. The two most frequent criticisms of him and his colleagues have been (1) that no one actually ever thought as the historian says he thought, and (2) where it is a case of literature, the history of ideas leaves literary value out of account. As for the first point, an historian is not writing psychology; and as for the second, he is not writing literary criticism or aesthetics. Nor had he, when he is in his right mind, any intention of doing either. We know too much about the influence of unconscious motivation on ideas to deny it, but that does not mean that a study of the development of the effect implies a denial of its having been caused. Similarly the fact that a novel or poem has great aesthetic value does not imply that it either has or does not have something to say. To discover German post-Kantian philosophy or traces of Neo-Platonism in Wordsworth or Emerson is to say nothing whatsoever about anything else which may be there, nor does such a discovery imply that either poet was or was not aware of the literary sources of what he was saying.

HAROLD CHERNISS

The History of Ideas and Ancient Greek
Philosophy

ᐳᐳᐳᐳᐳᐳᐳᐳᐳᐳᐳᐳᐳᐳᐳᐳᐳᐳᐳᐳᐳᐳᐳ

Both "history" and "idea" are Greek words, though the
meaning or meanings of the latter in Greek are so thoroughly
different from what is intended by it in ordinary English that
I prefer to avoid it except in its technical philosophical sense
and to use instead "thought," "concept," or "notion." "History," however, is not only a Greek word; the conception which
it is ordinarily meant to convey, the causal relations of events
to one another and the investigation of those relations, is a Greek
discovery or invention or, as some modern historiographers might
prefer to call it if they were aware of its origin, a figment of
Greek imagination and a manifestation of Greek prejudice in
favor of neat arrangements and rational systemization.

From the sixth century B. C. Greek thinkers were obsessed by
the desire to establish causal relations among all the entities and
events of which they had cognizance; and this activity, its objects
of whatever kind, and the resulting account which was supposed
to represent the objective system or process were all called ἱστορία.
"Blessed is he," says Euripides, "who has learned this ἱστορία,
contemplating the ageless order of immortal nature." [1] The early

---

[1] Euripides, fragment 910 (Nauck); cf. for the use of ἱστορία, Diels, Dox.
Graec., p. 102, n. 2, and Wyttenbach Ad Platonis Phaedonem 96 A (Platonis
Phaedon, editio auctior [1830], pp. 256-57).

22

" philosophers," as we call them by retrojection of the term, were all "historians" in this sense, "investigators" not merely of cosmogony, inanimate physical processes, biology, and psychology, but also of anthropology and of social and political events, ancient and contemporary. Of their works we have only exiguous fragments and reports at second-hand or third; but evidence enough exists to show that even the Ionians, the earliest of the " pre-Socratics," were not exclusively " natural historians " or "physiologers" and that probably all—and certainly some— of them treated the physical origin of things as only the first chapter in their investigation of the causes of the world of men in which they lived. Did they, then, extend this investigation to the origins and the alterations of men's beliefs and opinions and attempt to construct a genealogy, to use one of their own metaphors,[2] of thoughts and of the words which express thought and influence it in turn? Had they, in short, conceived the notion even in a crude and primitive fashion of what is here called " the history of ideas "?

Certainly they were keenly aware of the multiplicity and difference of human customs and opinions, the sort of diversity which in the physical world seemed to them to demand an explanation. Hecataeus of Miletus [3] began his history with the statement that he was about to write the truth as he saw it, for the accounts given by the Greeks were many and absurd; and Hecataeus in turn was used by Heraclitus [4] along with Xenophanes, Pythagoras, and Hesiod to support by way of example his contention that much learning does not produce understanding. The extant remains of most of these early writers contain equally sharp

---

[2] Cf. Heidel, *Anaximander's Book*, p. 263, n. 62, and Aelian, *V. H.* IV, 17 (quoted by Schuhl, *Essai sur la Formation de la Pensée Grecque*, p. 148, n. 1).

[3] Frag. 332 (Müller) = 1a (Jacoby [I, p. 7]).

[4] 22 B 40 (Diels-Kranz).

censure of the doctrines of their predecessors and of the opinions of the many. Xenophanes, who apparently adopted an extreme position of empirical common sense in opposition to all subtle "scientific theory," scornfully called the wars of the gods with the Titans and the Giants "fictions of the men of old." [5] Heraclitus, who expressed complete contempt for the multitude which followed false teachers and for the "polymaths" alike because they did not perceive the true "logos," received from Parmenides the supreme indignity of having the terms of his "logos" used to describe the men who wander in utter ignorance, facing both ways and believing that to be and not to be are the same thing and not the same.[6] All the processes which men believe to be real Parmenides declared to be nothing but words which they had themselves established; [7] and Empedocles, berating men for supposing that anything could come to be or be destroyed, adapted to his own use the charge of Parmenides that these supposed processes are mere misnomers.[8]

Such censure is not balanced by acknowledgment of any debt to earlier thinkers, even the obvious one of stimulation. This might be an incidental result of the ravages of time which have left us so little of what the pre-Socratics wrote, but the tone of what has been preserved to us makes any such generous explanation at least improbable. Heraclitus boasted that he had "made research into himself," that is to say that he had learned from no one else but had found the truth by introspection.[9] This way he must have considered to be open to anyone who has the will

---

[5] Frag. 1 (I, p. 128, 2 [Diels-Kranz]).

[6] Frag. 6 (I, p. 233, 4-9 [Diels-Kranz]).

[7] Frag. 8, 38-41 (I, p. 238, 7-10 [Diels-Kranz]).

[8] Frag. 11 (I, p. 313, 18-20 [Diels-Kranz]) and Frag. 8 (I, p. 312, 7-10 [Diels-Kranz]).

[9] Frag. 101 (I, p. 173, 11 [Diels-Kranz]) and A 1, § 5 (I, p. 140, 23-24 [Diels-Kranz]).

to take it, for he asserted that intelligent thought is common to all; [10] and, though he upbraided humanity for taking poets and the mob to be its instructors, [11] he ascribed the diversity and falsity of men's opinions to the fact that they turn away from the common "logos" each to illusory thoughts of his own, [12] as men in sleep turn each to a private world away from the single cosmos that they share while waking. [13] Empedocles explained the multitude of erroneous doctrines as the result of "partial views" of the truth: each individual, having seen but a small part of the whole, is convinced that what he has chanced upon in his little life is everything; [14] and this explanation he applied [15] specifically to the "common sense" statement of Xenophanes [16] that the earth extends downwards to infinity.

These accounts have more affinity with theories of knowledge, however, than they have with any theory of the interrelation or development of thoughts, opinions, or doctrines. The germ of such a theory might more plausibly be recognized in a fragment of the unphilosophical Xenophanes, [17] which says that the gods did not reveal all things to mortals from the beginning but men by seeking discover in time what is better. This is an early, perhaps the earliest expression of the theory of intellectual and cultural progress which later became a common-place of Greek

[10] Frag. 113 (I, 176, 4 [Diels-Kranz]).

[11] Frag. 104 (I, p. 174, 3-6 [Diels-Kranz]) and Frag. 57 (I, p. 163, 7-9 [Diels-Kranz].

[12] Frag. 2 (I, p. 151, 1-4 [Diels-Kranz]).

[13] Frag. 89 (I, p. 171, 3-5 [Diels-Kranz]); cf. Frag. 72 (I, p. 167, 9-11) which suggests that Heraclitus intended the proportion: the unintelligent awake are like men asleep, i. e., the intelligent: the unintelligent awake = the unintelligent awake: men asleep.

[14] Frag. 2 (I, p. 309, 2-6 [Diels-Kranz]).

[15] Frag. 39 (I, p. 329, 5-7 [Diels-Kranz]).

[16] Frag. 28 (I, p. 135, 16-17 [Diels-Kranz]).

[17] Frag. 18 (I, p. 133, 13-14 [Diels-Kranz]).

thought; [18] and positivistic interpreters, combining this fragment with one which they took to express a doctrine of scepticism,[19] have ascribed to Xenophanes the adumbration of their own notions of the nature of scientific progress. It is tempting to assume that the fragment which I have cited involves the notion that each discovery or invention is in some way determined by those which preceded it; but there is no indication that Xenophanes was aware of this implication, and, even if he was, it is a long step from such a notion to the doctrine that there is any similar causal connection among men's thoughts and opinions. Xenophanes seems rather to have thought that in the sphere of the invisible and intangible there is an objective truth which different men may approximate in different degrees but can never and with certainty grasp as it is, since each infects it with his own fancy.[20] He had observed that different peoples ascribed different appearances to the gods and moreover that each created the gods in its own image, the Ethiopians making them black and snubnosed, the Thracians blue-eyed and red-haired; and he indicated the universality of this tendency by saying that the brute beasts, if they could draw or mould figures, would each give the gods shapes like their own. From this he concluded that the ascription of any human shape, characteristic, or activity to divinity is a subjective error of men, though he did not on the same grounds reject the notion of divinity itself. On the contrary, he asserted the unity of divinity, the nature of which he

[18] Cf. for example Isocrates, *Paneg.* § 32; Chaeremon, frag. 21 (Nauck[2], p. 788) ; Moschion, frag. 6 (Nauck[2], pp. 813 f.) which is particularly interesting because in lines 20-21 the three explanations of progress in time are mentioned: 1) the concern of Prometheus (i. e. gift of a higher power), 2) necessity, 3) nature as a result of long habit; Lucretius, V, 783 ff., especially 1105 ff.

[19] Frag. 34 (I, p. 137, 2-5 [Diels-Kranz]) ; cf. Shorey, *Class. Phil.*, VI (1911), pp. 88 ff. on Gomperz's interpretation.

[20] Frag. 34 (I, p. 137, 2-5 [Diels-Kranz]) ; cf. Wilamowitz, *Hermes*, LXI (1926) , p. 280, and the article of Fränkel there referred to.

ascertained through a primitive kind of negative theology by stripping away all the diverse human opinions concerning it.[21] There is no evidence to show whether or not he thought of generalizing this method of using diverse opinions to cancel one another and taking the residuum as the nearest possible approximation to truth; but in any case he did not attempt to explain the subjectivity even of theological belief further than by citing the transference to the gods of the forms, habits, and functions of their votaries, and he treated all the various opinions as being on the same level without attempting to establish any causal connection among them.

The diversity or diffusion of religious beliefs, of customs, and of what may be called the instruments or manifestations of culture did, however, widely engage the attention of early Greek investigators, who in their speculations treated the phenomena chiefly from the point of view of origins. An example is the case of the alphabet, which according to Greek tradition was the invention of Palamedes. Hecataeus[22] " corrected " this tradition by saying that Danaus had brought the alphabet to Greece, which is to say that the Greek alphabet came from Egypt. Herodotus[23] later argued that it was brought into Greece by the Phoenicians and borrowed first by Ionians who made some changes in it. Thereafter almost everyone had his own special thesis to defend in regard to this problem.

What concerns our present interest is, however, the assump-

[21] Frags. 11-16 (I, pp. 132-33 [Diels-Kranz]) and Frags. 23-26 (I, p. 135 [Diels-Kranz]) .

[22] Cf. *Scholia in Dionysii Thracis Artem Grammaticam,* p. 183, 5-9 (Hilgard). The Anaximander mentioned along with Hecataeus is probably the younger man of this name (cf. Jacoby, *Fr. Gr. Hist.* 9 F 3, I, p. 160) , although Kleingünther (ΠΡΩΤΟΣ ΕΥΡΕΤΗΣ, pp. 40, 45, 64) assumes that he is the Milesian philosopher.

[23] Herodotus, V, 57-59; cf. Kleingünther, *op. cit.,* pp. 60-64.

tion common to all of them that the existence of writing in different languages in different countries must be explained by the direct transfer of writing from one to another, the consequent assumption of a single original writing, and the tendency to identify by personal names the agents of the invention and of the transfers. It sounds late and strange when one hears the scholiast on Dionysius Thrax [24] say that the probability is that there were inventors of alphabets in every land and that this explains why the characters used by different peoples are different. Such a notion of independent discoveries or inventions of similar instruments or customs seems never to have occurred to earlier writers such as Hecataeus; [25] and certainly the possibility is never suggested in the many passages of Herodotus which deal with these matters. In them a unique origin is always assumed even in the unusual case in which Herodotus cannot make up his mind what the origin of a widespread custom is,[26] and in this case as always it is assumed that the Greeks, if they share the custom or use the instrument, are the borrowers, not the originators of it. So, to mention but a few examples and those which concern intellectual history, it was from Egypt that the Greeks got geometry,[27] the belief in metempsychosis,[28] and the names of most of the gods, these last having come by way of the Pelasgians who devised the few that did not come originally from Egypt.[29]

This search for origins, which in the extant literature we can first observe being pursued over a wide field in the history of Herodotus, though there are indications of its practice at a

---

[24] *Scholia in Dionysii Thracis Artem Grammaticam*, p. 183, 16-17 (Hilgard)
[25] Cf. Kleingünther, *op. cit.*, p. 46.
[26] II, 167; cf. Kleingünther, *op. cit.*, p. 53 and pp. 57 ff.
[27] II, 109, 3.
[28] II, 123.
[29] II, 4, 2; 50; 52-53.

much earlier date, was systematized in the form of catalogues of
" Heuremata " which appeared first under Sophistic influence at
the end of the fifth century and issued finally in the Peripatetic
collection entited " Peplos." [30]

The observation of diverse human customs and beliefs impelled
Greek thought at the same time in another direction, a direction
clearly indicated by the implications which Xenophanes had seen
in the diverse forms of the various national gods. Herodotus,
who so assiduously and confidently sought the unique origin of
similar customs, gave remarkable expression to this other tendency also. Cambyses, he wrote,[31] in scoffing at the religious
customs of the Egyptians, showed plainly that he was violently
mad, for, if one should propose to all men that they choose the
fairest customs of all, each group after examining all would
choose its own; and in support of this statement he tells the
story of the Greeks and Indians who were outraged by the
impious suggestion that either group should dispose of its dead
in the way that the other considered pious. Before Herodotus,
Pindar had put the point succinctly: " Different customs are
current with different people, and each one lauds his own
justice." [32] What implication Pindar saw in this is not known,
since the fragment is preserved in isolation; the moral that
Herodotus drew was tolerance of differences of belief, but the
seed of this tolerance could as easily flower in complete cynicism.
If the diversity of opinions about the form of the gods had not
brought Xenophanes to atheism, it had seemed to him to prove
that *all* the various opinions on the subject were erroneous.
Heraclitus may have thought that he had discovered a sanction
for the diverse customs of different men when he made the

[30] Cf. Kleingünther, *op. cit.*, pp. 146-51.
[31] III, 38.
[32] Frag. 203 (Bowra) = 215 (Schroeder).

pronouncement that all human laws are nourished by the one divine law;[33] but he had at the same time emphasized the distinction which was to lead to the conviction that the very diversity of human laws and customs proved them all to be equally arbitrary, artificial, and invalid, all opposed to true or natural morality rather than different manifestations or aspects of it. So it came that Sophocles could make Antigone in the height of moral fervor appeal against the statutes of the state to " the unwritten statutes which live not for today or yesterday but forever and no-one knows their beginning." [34]

To the men of the " sophistic enlightenment," the diversity of human customs implied no such higher " unwritten statute " which all men are bound in conscience to obey but the relativity and artificiality of all law and custom and an incompatibility between these conventions and nature. " Matters of law or custom," said Antiphon,[35] " are adventitious, but the rules of nature are necessary; the former are the results of convention and do not arise of themselves, whereas the latter grow of themselves and are not conventional. . . . Most of what is just according to law is inimical to nature." Since customs came to be regarded as human contrivances, it was assumed that they had been contrived by particular human beings, even though these individuals could no longer be identified by name, as Critias [36] assumed that there had been some single individual who had contrived the notion of religion and had persuaded men to adopt it. This tendency and, what is more important, the kind of ethical arguments in support of which it was used, appear in parody at the

[33] Frag. 114 (I, p. 176, 5-9 [Diels-Kranz]) .

[34] *Antigone* 456-57.

[35] *Oxyrh. Pap.* XI, no. 1364 ed. Hunt, Frag. A, cols. 1-2 (II, pp. 346-48 [Diels-Kranz]) .

[36] Frag. 25 (II, pp. 386-89 [Diels-Kranz]) , lines 12 and 41-42.

end of Aristophanes' *Clouds*,[37] where when the father, objecting to being beaten by his son, argues:

On beating fathers custom everywhere has placed its ban,

the son replies:

Was not the one who first devised this custom then a man
Like you and me, and did he not by speech persuade the
    crowd
In olden times; and am I any less to be allowed
To set up a new custom for the future age to learn
That sires who once their children whipped be flogged by
    them in turn?

And for good measure he adds an argument which parodies the opposition of nature to convention and the theory, adopted by Democritus,[38] that men learned the arts and crafts by imitating the lower animals:

Look to the cocks and all the other beasts that you can
    name.
They knock their fathers all about; and yet they're just the
    same
As we are, save that they don't play the legislative game.[39]

Reflection upon the diversity of scientific or philosophical theory and opinion led to a conclusion similar to that which was reached by such reflection in the sphere of law and custom and culminated in the intellectual nihilism of Gorgias and the intellectual relativism of Protagoras. One might have expected the Sophists to exploit not merely the diversity of scientific opinions but the possibility of an aetiology and history of such opinions in order to support their scepticism in this field in the way that they sought to establish it in the ethical and social

---

[37] 1420-24.
[38] Frag. 154 (II, p. 173, 11-15 [Diels-Kranz]).
[39] *Clouds*, 1427-29.

spheres; but no indication exists that they saw this opportunity or in any way tried to construct a causal relation among the opinions and theories which they played off against one another for the purpose of discrediting all.

Besides the attempts to identify origins and originators there is in the extant pre-Platonic literature evidence for only one other kind of historical treatment of philosophical or scientific opinions. Democritus [40] in his " Little Diacosmos " said that the theories concerning the sun and moon which Anaxagoras had put forward were not his own but had been stolen by him from earlier thinkers. A fragment of Heraclitus,[41] the authenticity of which is doubtful, charges Pythagoras in similar fashion with having excerpted the writings of others and having claimed the resulting wisdom as his own. The charge of plagiarism may at first sight appear to have little to do with the history of ideas; but like the catalogues of " Heuremata " it became one of the accepted formulae used by post-Aristotelian historians of philosophy and, like other formulae in the history of human thought, was ultimately taken so seriously that it became a motive for altering the evidence to account for which it was originally set up. The ironical historian may be amused to observe that Democritus was himself charged by an Epicurean writer with having plagiarized the " Great Diacosmos " of Leucippus,[42] whose very existence Epicurus himself denied.[43] To cite only one other example, Plato was accused of having plagiarized the writings of Protagoras [44] and of Philolaus; [45] and on the strength of another version of this hypothesis the " original "

[40] Frag. 5 (II, p. 134, 7-10 [Diels-Kranz]) .

[41] Frag. 129 (I, p. 180, 13 ff. [Diels-Kranz]) .

[42] 67 B 1 a (II, p. 80, 7 ff. [Diels-Kranz]) .

[43] Cf. Bailey, *The Greek Atomists and Epicurus*, p. 66.

[44] 80 B 2 and 5 (II, p. 264, 12-19, and p. 265, 13 ff. [Diels-Kranz]) .

[45] 44 A 1 (I, p. 398, 13-18 [Diels-Kranz]) .

from which he was supposed to have copied the *Timaeus* was later forged and is still extant.[46] The motives for these later charges of plagiarism were, of course, various and complicated, and among them were often malice and the professional zeal of rival schools; but it is important to understand that the formula sometimes covered what we should now call the *influence* of one writer upon another and that in such cases it is only one example of the crude externalization of the history of ideas, of which the formula of " Heuremata " is another.

What Plato did with this formula of " Heuremata " is an instructive introduction to his attitude towards the history of thought in general. In the *Phaedrus* [47] Socrates gives an account of the invention of writing, ascribing it to Theuth, one of the gods who inhabited Egypt in ancient times, and telling how Thamous, the king, explained to the inventor that his invention would have effects the contrary of what he expected. It is for the sake of Thamous's criticism, of course, that Socrates tells this story of the invention which he introduces as an Egyptian tradition; but to make this perfectly clear Plato has at the end given Phaedrus and Socrates a brief interchange of remarks which defines his own conception of the limits and uses of such historical categories. The sophisticated, young Phaedrus knows that the story is not " historically true "; and his immediate comment at its conclusion is: " Socrates, you lightly invent tales of Egyptians and men of whatsoever land you like." Socrates replies that the generation of Phaedrus is wiser than the men of old who in their simplicity were satisfied with the truth even if it came from stocks and stones, whereas to Phaedrus it matters *who* has said a thing since his concern is not solely whether

---

[46] Timaeus Locrus, περὶ ψυχᾶς κόσμω καὶ φύσιος. (cf. Harder, *R.E.*, Zweite Reihe, VI, 1, 1223).
[47] 274C-275C.

what is said is true. This obviously is not merely what the commentators say, a warning to readers not to take Socrates' history as literally true; it is also Plato's confession that to him the importance of a theory or judgment lies in its meaning and validity and not in its author or origin; but it is besides Plato's apology for his own technique of presenting in the form of temporal history matters which he believes in truth transcend temporality. Here is, instead of the unconscious and naïve externalization of the history of thought, the conscious avowal of externalization as a technique of analysis and representation with the concomitant warning that the representation is not the truth but only a symbol of it.

The warning is repeated more explicitly in the *Timaeus*,[48] where Plato apologizes for describing in temporal sequence the creation of the material and spiritual factors of the universe and says that this manner of speaking is a consequence of the contingent or haphazard which is a large element in the constitution of man. The very form of expression which Plato chose to use, the dialogue, is an application of this technique of externalization, the externalization of thought which is the dialogue of the soul with itself, the different moments represented by different characters whose names are historical names and whose masks and tones are so realistically portrayed that great scholars have insisted that this must all be history—not a fiction of Plato's but the veritable words of Socrates and his companions and opponents faithfully recorded. All the more difficult has it been for readers to understand in what sense those passages of the dialogues are historical which profess to deal with the interrelation of the doctrines of earlier philosophers.

There is a famous passage in the *Phaedo* [49] in which Socrates

[48] 34C.   [49] 96 A ff.

tells how in his youth he zealously engaged in the investigation of nature, hoping to learn the causes of things, how the various doctrines of earlier philosophers, unnamed but identifiable, left him more bewildered than ever, how his hopes were raised when he heard of Anaxagoras' doctrine of Νοῦς and were dashed again when he read the book of Anaxagoras, and how finally in desperation he took refuge in his own method of dialectic and in the theory of ideas. This passage has been taken by some scholars quite literally as an historical account of Socrates' development, and in the references to the various doctrines mentioned they have tried to identify the historical influences upon Socrates' thought; but then one must also take the culminating theory of ideas as the doctrine of Socrates, not of Plato, and all the evidence that we have—and there is much of it—speaks against this.[50] Did Plato then intend this to be his own intellectual autobiography transferred to Socrates? Only in the sense that it is neither the one nor the other exclusively but a generalized " philosopher's progress," and a " philosopher's progress " in which the progressive stages are represented by particular doctrines of earlier philosophy arranged according to a schematic interpretation.

The philosopher symbolized by Socrates begins with a dim perception of that which this progress is to clarify. He seeks the causes of things, αἱ αἰτίαι which he specifies at the beginning as " the cause *why*," διὰ τί,[51] without yet being aware of the implications of that specification. First he seeks in vain through the different mechanistic theories, which are arranged schematically and not according to their historical chronological

---

[50] One of the interesting bits of evidence is *Metaphysics* 987 B 31-33, an obvious reminiscence of *Phaedo* 99 E ff., which shows that Aristotle took the last part of this "biography of Socrates" as a reference to Plato, not to Socrates.

[51] 96 A 8-10.

sequence and among which is included the mechanistic part of Anaxagoras' doctrine,[52] the author of which is not named, because his doctrine has been divided in two in order that the nonmechanistic part with which his name is especially connected may be used to represent the second stage. It is only after the philosopher has been disappointed in the promise which that part of Anaxagoras' doctrine, the conception of Νοῦς, seemed to him to make that he understands why the doctrines of the earlier stage only increased his bewilderment, for now because of the suggestion of Anaxagoras which Anaxagoras did not himself understand he can clarify that cause as διὰ τί which he was seeking from the beginning and see that it is final causality as distinguished from necessary condition, which, Socrates now says,[53] most people, like men who fumble for their way in the dark, mistakenly give the name of " cause."

This brief analysis of the passage shows, I think, that, while Plato is here concerned with the interrelation of philosophical theories and employs for the elements of his construction doctrines which were held by historical persons, his purpose is not to give an account of the development of any particular individual or of the whole of preceding philosophy. He has put into the temporal sequence of a narrative what he considered to be the necessary relation of the various possible ways of looking at the problem of causality; and, although the whole " progress " culminates in the theory of ideas, we cannot assume even that it therefore describes, or that Plato meant it to describe, the course by which he arrived at that theory himself.

So Plato intended something other than what we mean by an historical account when in the *Theaetetus* [54] he wrote that, with the exception of Parmenides, all the wise men in succession

---

[52] 96 C 7-D 3.   [53] 99 A-B.   [54] 152 E ff.

from Homer, the father of tragedy, and Epicharmus, the father
of comedy, are to be taken as agreeing on the proposition that
nothing ever exists but all things are always in process of
becoming and gives by name as examples of these wise men
Protagoras, Heraclitus, and Empedocles. He did undoubtedly
intend most seriously to emphasize that the relativism which in
this dialogue he elaborated and in its elaborated form put into
the mouth of Protagoras had always been one aspect of Greek
thought or perhaps had always been and would always be one
aspect of all human thought. To the external form, however,
in which he expressed this interpretation he ascribed no validity
of its own. That is clear from the fact that he altered this form
to suit different contexts, as when in the *Cratylus* [55] he made
Socrates profess to discover the doctrine of Heraclitus in lines
of Homer, Hesiod, and Orpheus and even to ascribe it to the
hypothetical founders of language but made no mention of
Protagoras, Empedocles, or Epicharmus. When one recalls, moreover, the opinion expressed by Socrates in the *Protagoras* [56]
concerning the use and possibility of discovering what the poets
really meant, one cannot suppose that Plato would have seriously
defended the interpretations by means of which he read into
Homer's lines the doctrine of flux or relativity. Whether or not
Homer really espoused that doctrine consciously or at all did
not concern him; he believed that the attitude towards reality
of which that doctrine is a manifestation was as old as thought
itself, he wanted a symbol by means of which he could most
vividly express that belief, and so he used Homer as such a
symbol, nothing more.

It is for the same reason that in the *Sophist* [57] the Eleatic
doctrine of the unity of being is said to have " begun with

---

[55] 401 B-402 D.   [56] 347 C-348 A.   [57] 242 D-E.

Xenophanes and even earlier." The opposite of the notion that being is many must have been as old as that notion. Not only Empedocles, who was later in time than Parmenides, but Heraclitus, too, who was certainly earlier, is there represented as having sought a compromise between these two extremes; and it may be that it was in order to avoid an obvious anachronism that the name of Parmenides is not mentioned along with that of Xenophanes in this passage. This is not to say that Plato here "rearranged" history; he was not interested in history at all in the sense of the temporal sequence of theories. In his opinion the tendencies towards the many and the one and compromise between them are always present in human thought, and the logical scheme into which he analyses this nontemporal fact misrepresents that fact no more than does the historical externalization of the truth in time—or rather not so much.

This difference between Plato's attitude and ours towards the history of thought is most strikingly exemplified by a later passage in the *Sophist* [58] in which he describes as a battle of the giants the argument between the materialists and "the friends of the ideas," the former dragging all things down to earth and insisting that only what can be touched and felt has existence, the latter defending themselves from some invisible height and maintaining that intelligible and incorporeal ideas are true existence. "Between them," Plato says, "is joined forever war without limit." Modern scholars almost without exception [59] have assumed that the two parties here described must have been historical persons, whom they have forthwith attempted not without much controversy to identify. Certain characteristics ascribed to either later in the passage do make it possible to ascertain the particular groups that Plato used as his models for

[58] 246 A ff.
[59] There are some exceptions, chief among them Paul Friedländer.

the descriptions; but Plato has said that the struggle continues forever, and so the historical persons whose particular lineaments of argument and designation were borrowed for the description or even perhaps suggested it are not what was significant to him but only served as symbols of two factions which he saw always at strife in human thought.

Such considerations did not occur to Aristotle, who apparently supposed that Plato had intended his schematic analyses for "history." So Plato's use of Homer caused him to consider in all gravity whether the poet had really been a physical philosopher before Thales and had anticipated the latter's doctrine.[60] Upon this question he pronounced a "*non liquet*"; but Plato's similar use of Xenophanes he not only took in the same literal fashion but accepted in this sense as true, so that in virtue of this misconception Xenophanes became the founder of the Eleatic school and the teacher of Parmenides.[61] Examples like this indicate that Aristotle failed to understand Plato's purposely unhistorical technique; but for all that his own method of treating earlier thought is not without some similarity to Plato's and was not unaffected by it.

Such a statement as this may at first hearing seem to be both paradoxical and heretical. The most learned historian of Greek philosophy has paid homage to the historical research and erudition of Aristotle and has called him the originator of the history of philosophy; [62] and Aristotle's treatment of his predecessors in his extant works is so extensive and detailed that large parts of his writings do sound like histories of philosophy and, read by themselves, give the impression of having been written with what we should call a purely historical purpose. Almost every phi-

---

[60] *Metaphysics* 983 B 27-984 A 2; cf. Ross, *Metaphysics* I, p. 130.
[61] *Metaphysics* 986 B 21 ff.; cf. Ross, *op. cit.*, p. 153.
[62] Zeller, *Phil. Griech.*, I, 2, p. 1361.

losophical question that he discusses is introduced by an account of the earlier treatments of the question; and these are usually presented not as mere lists of different opinions but as doctrines which in their origins and their peculiar characteristics are somehow related to one another. The explanation, for example, in *Metaphysics* A of the influences which were responsible for Plato's formulation of the theory of ideas [63] and in the essay on *Generation and Corruption* [64] the account of the background and origins of the atomic theory sound as if they might have been written by a modern historian and have in fact been reproduced as satisfactory and accurate accounts by most historians of Greek philosophy.

When it is observed, however, that in different contexts Aristotle gives different accounts of the same doctrine, omitting or emphasizing different parts of it, finding in it different and even incompatible meanings and implications, and explaining its origins and background in quite different ways, and especially when it is further observed that such variations are always relevant to some particular part of his own philosophical doctrine, the establishment of which constitutes the larger context,[65] it becomes clear that these expositions were written for a purpose that was not merely historical and that the character of each exposition and interpretation was determined by this purpose.

Aristotle was certainly influenced by the literary form in which Plato had written, for he wrote dialogues himself; but, since none of these survives, it cannot be known whether they were more than superficial imitations of the form of Plato's literary expression. It may be the effect of this same influence in a pro-

[63] *Metaphysics* 987 A 32-B 10.
[64] *De Generatione* 324 B 35-325 B 15.
[65] See Cherniss, *Aristotle's Criticism of Presocratic Philosophy, passim,* e. g. pp. 220-21, p. 113, and Chapter VII, e. g. p. 349.

founder sense, however, that so much of the extant technical writing of Aristotle consists of aporetic discussions. Each of these discussions is a kind of dialogue in which the interlocutors are replaced by the expositions of earlier opinions which are played off against one another. Each opinion is meant to contribute to the conclusion of the discussion, which is Aristotle's own doctrine; and this end determines the choice and interpretation of the opinions of his predecessors in each particular context. The purpose of his expositions of earlier thought was, then, dialectical rather than historical; but the justification of this dialectical technique lay in his conception of the history of thought. He believed that the full truth had been discovered and lost many times, that his own system was the completion of one of these cycles of discovery, and that all previous doctrines known to him were vague and confused vestiges of the truth and therefore " stammering " attempts to express his own system. These earlier doctrines were then the material from which by combination and interpretation the shattered pattern of reality could be reintegrated; [66] conversely, the only rule by which earlier doctrines could be judged, compared, and distinguished must be the extent to which they succeeded in approximating the norm which was Aristotle's system, and he groups and regroups them to emphasize now one phase of this theory and again another. Even the exposition of previous philosophy which constitutes the whole of the first book of the *Metaphysics* is in fact a dialectical argument in support of the Aristotelian doctrine of the four types of causality and was intended as such.

" It is evident," Aristotle says in conclusion of this exposition,[67] " that all men seem to seek the causes named in the *Physics* and

---

[66] Cf. *Aristotle's Criticism of Presocratic Philosophy*, p. 348 and references there.

[67] *Metaphysics* 993 A 11 ff.

that we cannot name any besides these; but they seek them vaguely; and, though in a sense they have all been described before, in a sense they have not been described at all, for early philosophy is on all subjects like one that lisps, in that it is young and in its beginnings." In final exemplification of this he explains that Empedocles, though he did not clearly state the position for which his doctrine is here employed, would necessarily have agreed with the Aristotelian clarification of it, had this been put before him. Aristotle did not envisage the possibility that the problems with which earlier thinkers were concerned may have been different from his own. He was concerned with their opinions as varying approximations to an expression of the truth which is identical for all; and, if at times his treatment of them has to us more the semblance of history than Plato's has, that is chiefly because this truth, which he conceived as the final cause of all these philosophical opinions, was no longer as for Plato an extratemporal world of ideas but his own philosophical system, the expression of which did follow them in time as the full flowering of what they contained in seed and had manifested only partially and imperfectly.

Yet Aristotle, even if he was not an historian of philosophy, was in a different sense the founder of the history of philosophy. His pupils or associates in the Lyceum were encouraged or perhaps incited by him to undertake historical researches in many fields, among the most famous and influential of which were Aristoxenus' *History of Music*, Eudemus' *History of Mathematics*, and Theophrastus' *History of Natural Philosophy*. Much of this Peripatetic work was purely annalistic or what we should call compilations of the materials for history rather than historical writing. At the same time there was cultivated among the Peripatetics a taste for biography which from the very beginning leaned strongly towards the scandalous. From the work of

Theophrastus descended all the later so-called doxographical writings, summaries more or less elaborate of the opinions of philosophers arranged in encyclopaedic fashion either by subjects or by schools, with later additions by hands only conjecturally identifiable. In them and in the extant fragments of the *History* of Theophrastus from which they are ultimately descended can be discerned a certain influence of Aristotle, for which Aristotle cannot be fairly held responsible. The dialectical configurations and interpretations which he had employed were taken for literal history by Theophrastus even as Aristotle had sometimes taken literally the dialectical schemata of Plato. Moreover, Theophrastus began to use as a regular expedient to explain apparent similarities in the opinions and formulations of different thinkers the assumption of a teacher-pupil relation and the framework of philosophical schools, a construction to which Aristotle had already occasionally had recourse and which later became a highly elaborated device of the historians. It is but one example, though the most obvious and striking one, of the ever increasing externalization of the history of philosophy from this point onwards in ancient times; the extremes to which it was driven may be seen in the first book of Diogenes Laertius [68] where all philosophers down to Clitomachus, Chrysippus, Theophrastus, and Epicurus—that is, Academic, Stoic, Peripatetic, and Epicurean—are fitted into two schools deriving by direct lines of succession from Thales and Pherecydes.

From the Hellenistic Age onwards, histories of philosophy were written that were divorced from all philosophizing; but in consequence they were nothing more than lists of philosophical opinions or sequences of biographies of philosophers consisting largely of personal anecdotes, and even those opinions and these

---

[68] I, 13-15.

biographical details were usually derived not from the original writings of the philosophers concerned or even from serious historical records but by multiple reflection from the dialectical passages of Aristotle, from the fictionalized or scandalous Peripatetic biographies, or from such dialogues and philosophical romances as those of Heraclides Ponticus, Aristoxenus, Clearchus, and Eratosthenes. The sediment of all this writing is preserved for us in the undigested, uncritical, and often self-contradictory collection of Diogenes Laertius entitled *The Lives and Opinions of the Eminent Philosophers*, which, because it is·unique, having outlived all its sources, has served as the foundation of all modern histories of Greek philosophy.

The philosophers, when they dealt with earlier thought at all, did so either to repudiate it all in establishment of their own absolute originality, as did Epicurus, or to read into some earlier writer their own doctrines, as the Stoics did with Heraclitus or as Plotinus did with Plato. Dissatisfaction with the multiplicity of philosophical dogmas gave rise to syncretism, which operated by compromising the differences among divergent doctrines, or to scepticism, which mustered all known differences of opinion concerning every possible question in order to prove that no certain knowledge is attainable concerning anything; but neither the syncretists nor the sceptics attempted to explain how such differences of opinion arose or to relate them to one another or to circumstances and conditions which might have determined them. In short, there is not anywhere in Greek philosophy or the Greeks' own history of philosophy anything that corresponds to what we call the history of ideas.

Why Plato and Aristotle were not concerned with the history of thought as mere history I have already indicated. They were concerned with something else, with the nature of objective truth, with the ideas or universals which have no history rather than with the particular attempts of particular human beings to formulate in thought or speech the nature of this eternal truth. When they sought, each in his own way, to formulate the nature of this truth or to indicate the procedure by which it could be grasped (for Plato's writings at least have rather the latter purpose than the former), they made use of historical names and formulations, to be sure, but they used them as material to be reshaped by their dialectical method with the intention not of accurately retracing the particular course that thought had taken in the past but of eliciting the typical or universal aspects from these imperfect particular manifestations, Plato fashioning an ideal panorama of philosophy, the moments of which must always be present in human thinking as the problem of the one and the many, he says,[69] is a deathless and ageless affection of human discourse which had no beginning and will never have an end, Aristotle refashioning historical material as tragedy refashions it in order to state not what has happened but what may happen, whereby it is more philosophical than history is.[70] To Aristotle as well as to Plato the very possibility of what we call a history of ideas would have seemed to be incompatible with philosophy, which to them implied an objective and eternal truth discernible by each individual human mind directly.

Something of this attitude was characteristic of all Greek philosophical thought. The doctrine of the relativity of sensation so widely held by the pre-Socratics was not extended by them to knowledge and the object of knowledge; Heraclitus, Parmenides, and Empedocles all assumed an objective truth, the knowledge of which is possible directly and only directly to each individual, and even the Atomists and Epicureans, whose theory

[69] *Philebus* 15 D.
[70] *Poetics* 1451 B 4 ff.

of the origin of the arts in human imitation of the other animals could have been extended into a theory of the growth and development of human thought, made no such extension of it themselves but explained the mental state and knowledge of each individual independently by the varying impact upon each of the atoms which for them constituted the unique objective truth. The case of Protagoras and the later Sceptics is most instructive of all in this connection, for it might have been expected that, when they rejected the possibility of attaining objective truth, they would have explained the various opinions of men in terms of the influence upon men's minds of their linguistic, cultural, and philosophical environments and antecedents. This they did not do; but instead they left each man an autonomous world in himself, generating his own thoughts without relation to those of his predecessors. So pervasive was the notion that the thought of each individual is directed to a universal and objective truth of some kind and determined by it that people like this, who denied the existence or the accessibility of such truth, could not conceive of relating the thoughts of the individual to anything else unless it were to make them merely epiphenomena of sensation. To explain them as passing from mind to mind, growing, developing, changing, and vanishing to reappear later in altered guise or shifted intention would have seemed to them to be more mythological than Protagoras' avowed myth of Zeus's distribution of a sense of justice to men, for it would be to endow with life and individuality of their own what are only functions of individual minds. They did not have the successful hypothesis of biological evolution to make it easy for them to employ the metaphor of the growth, mutation, and development of ideas as such.

As for the biographers and doxographers, the ancient specialists in the history of philosophy, they wrote as recorders of events or scorekeepers without any critical understanding of the philosophical problems with which the subjects of their histories had wrestled, of the various techniques that had been employed to resolve these problems, or of the different ways in which the solutions had been determined by the status of the problems and the manner of grappling with them. In so far as they tried at all to explain the philosophy, the history of which they were supposedly writing, they did so by means of biographical accidents in the lives of the philosophers or by treating dogmas as counters passed from one column to another and added, subtracted, or exchanged against one another in the account-books of the schools. Of them no history of ideas could be expected, for they did not concern themselves with ideas but at best with an epitome of their expression and with the lives of those who had expressed them. Their work is useful to us only because most of the philosophy of which it pretends to be a history and is not has disappeared; but the limits of its usefulness are painfully strict and very dangerous to overstep, and its later influence even down to the present has been sinister, for the complete externalization of the history of ancient philosophy has been encouraged and maintained to a great extent by its example. There can be no real history of philosophy unless the historian philosophizes, philosophizes within the framework of his subject and at the same time keeps his critical faculty detached and vigilant over the philosophy which he is rethinking. That is why the ancient doxographers were not historians of ideas; it is why so much of the modern history of ancient philosophy is little better than doxography; but conversely, if I may be bold to give one reason for many, it is why the study of the history of ideas has been prosecuted with such sound and signal success by the man to whom we here express our gratitude, Professor Arthur O. Lovejoy.

LUDWIG EDELSTEIN

The Golden Chain of Homer

➤➤➤➤➤➤➤➤➤➤➤➤➤➤➤➤➤➤➤

In his admirable work *The Great Chain of Being*, Professor
Lovejoy has shown the importance which the concept of the
Scale of Being and its figurative expression, the chain, had for
Western thought from the early Middle Ages down to the
nineteenth century. In an introductory chapter he has outlined
the genesis of the idea itself in Greek philosophy. Yet, not pri-
marily concerned with the Greek development, he has refrained
from inquiring how far back in ancient literature one can trace
the metaphor, and by what process it became a phrase identified
with the Neo-Platonic theory of emanation. These questions I
propose to discuss here, taking as my point of departure the
passage in Macrobius' commentary on the *Somnium Scipionis*
(I, 14, 15) through which, as Professor Lovejoy says, probably
most medieval writers became acquainted with the simile of
the chain.[1]

Speaking of the Supreme God, Mind, Soul and their creation,
as well as of the creation of all subsequent things, Macrobius
identifies " Homer's golden chain, which God, he says, bade hang
down from heaven to earth " (*Homeri catena aurea, quam pen-
dere de caelo in terras deum iussisse commemorat*) with the continuous succession of all things degenerating to the very bottom

---

[1] A. O. Lovejoy, *The Great Chain of Being*[2] (1942), 63.

of the series, " a connection of parts, from the Supreme God down to the last dregs of things, mutually linked together and without a break " (*a summo deo usque ad ultimam rerum faecem una mutuis se vinculis religans et nusquam interrupta connexio*).[2] The identification is made quite casually, and one can hardly believe that Macrobius should have been the first to offer it. In general, he follows Neo-Platonic writers, and it would therefore seem natural to believe that he took this metaphor from the same sources. However, it does not occur in Plotinus, who uses the other comparison which Macrobius adduces in his context, namely the series of mirrors (*e. g. Enneads*, I, 1, 8); nor is the chain of Homer mentioned with similar connotations in the extant writings of Porphyry, Iamblichus, or Julian. Consequently, scholars have suggested that Macrobius must have borrowed the simile from a Neo-Platonic work now lost.[3]

This supposition may well be correct. Yet, even if Macrobius depended on an earlier Neo-Platonic author, it is unwarranted to assume, as is usually done, that the metaphor was original with the Neo-Platonists.[4] It was in fact employed at least as early as the first half of the second century after Christ. The rhetor, Aristides, in his speech *On Zeus* contends that all gods are endowed with an emanation of the power of the highest deity, the creator of the world, and, he continues, " in the manner of the chain of Homer everything is fastened upon Him and everything is suspended from Him, a chain much more beautiful than that golden chain or any other chain one might

---

[2] The translation is Professor Lovejoy's (*loc. cit.*).

[3] M. Schedler, *Die Philosophie des Macrobius und ihr Einfluss auf die Wissenschaft des christlichen Mittelalters*, in *Beiträge z. Gesch. d. Philosophie d. Mittelalters*, XIII, 1 (1916), 12.

[4] E. g. W. Leaf, *The Iliad*, I[2] (1900), *ad* VIII, v. 19; L. Preller-C. Robert, *Griechische Mythologie*, I[4] (1894), 108, note 1; cf. also below, n. 33.

imagine" (*In Jovem*, 15) .[5] Even granted that Macrobius gives a more elaborate picture of the chain, fundamentally the metaphor is used in the same sense by Macrobius as by Aristides. The latter, too, envisages a unity of unequal parts, a descending sequence of values (*ibid.*, 15–17). His description of the position of Zeus reflects the doctrine of Middle Platonism with its tendency to elevate the might of the one and supreme god and to unify the various realms of being under his leadership. At least to this eclectic system, then, one can trace the chain as a metaphor of the Scale of Being.[6]

Nor were the Middle Platonists the first to ascribe an exalted philosophical significance to the episode at the beginning of the eighth Book of the *Iliad* (vv. 1–40), where Zeus forbids the assembled gods and goddesses to meddle in the affairs of mortals, threatens them with dire punishment in case they disobey, and dares them to make trial of his strength in a rope-pulling contest, with a rope of gold to be suspended from heaven (v. 19) ;

---

[5] "Ὥστε καὶ θεῶν ὅσα φῦλα ἀπορροὴν τῆς Διὸς τοῦ πάντων πατρὸς δυνάμεως ἕκαστα ἔχει καὶ ἀτεχνῶς κατὰ τὴν Ὁμήρου σειρὰν ἅπαντα εἰς αὐτὸν ἀνήρτηται καὶ πάντα ἐξ αὐτοῦ ἐξῆπται, πολὺ καλλίων ἅλυσις ἢ κατὰ χρυσῆν τε καὶ εἴ τινα ἄλλην τις ἐπινοήσειεν (43 Keil). For the date of the speech (around 142/3 A. D.) , cf. J. Amann, *Die Zeusrede des Ailios Aristeides*, in *Tübinger Beiträge z. Altertumswissenschaft*, XII (1931) , 36. Aristides' statement is adduced in explanation of the chains mentioned in Proclus' hymns by F. Jacobs, *Animadversiones in Epigrammata Anthologiae Graecae*, X (1801) , 273; 277; cf. J. F. Boissonade, *Marini Vita Procli* (1814) , 121. The passage is also quoted as an example of allegorical interpretation by C. G. Heyne, *Homeri Carmina* V (1802), 417. In the later discussion of the subject it has apparently been forgotten.

[6] For the doctrine of Middle Platonism, cf. F. Ueberweg-K. Praechter, *Die Philosophie des Altertums*[12] (1926) , 524 ff.; R. E. Witt, *Albinus and the History of Middle Platonism* (1937) . Amann, *op. cit.*, 24-27, speaks only of the influence of Plato and of the Stoa on Aristides; but cf. E. and L. Edelstein, *Asclepius*, II (1945) , 107. Aristides' evaluation of the demiurge agrees with Albinus, *Didaskalikos*, ch. XII (p. 167, 18 ff.) , on which see Witt, *op. cit.*, 133 f.

for in Homer surely it is a rope, not a chain, that is referred to, and it is called golden " to show its poetical character " (*Scholia A, ad loc.*).[7] From the fifth century B. C. this passage seems to have been of singular importance to all allegorizers; the earlier interpretations, I suggest, gradually led up to the meaning which the Middle Platonists later discovered in the words of Homer.

Plato's mention of the golden rope is the oldest philosophical testimony that has survived. In his opinion, the poet indicates by the rope "nothing other than the sun, and reveals that so long as the heavens and the sun keep moving, all things divine and human remain safe; but if this motion were halted, bound as it were, all things would be destroyed and everything, as the saying goes, turned upside down" (*Theaetetus*, 153 c-d). The allegory, as it is formulated here, probably is of Heraclitean origin, although it was hardly restricted to that school, and Plato adapts it to his own purposes.[8] In his ironic manner, he blends physical and metaphysical speculations. Like the sun, the rope maintains the existence of the cosmos and of all its parts. But the sun also symbolizes movement, and eternal movement, one might say, is considered the rope, the bond, that holds

[7] *Scholia Graeca in Homeri Iliadem*, ed. G. Dindorf, I (1875), 269. Cf. Leaf's comment on v. 19. Ps. Plutarch, *De vita et poesi Homeri*, 18, attributes to Homer an analogical use of the term, and so do some of the other scholia, but this surely is a later misunderstanding. The game referred to is described by Eusthatius, *Commentarii in Homeri Iliadem*, p. 1111.

[8] For the Heraclitean origin of the allegory, cf. e. g. L. Campbell, *The Theaetetus of Plato*[2] (1883), *ad loc*. Euripides (*Orestes*, v. 982) calls the sun a rock held in suspense between heaven and earth by golden "chains" (ἀλύσεσιν). The expression may be derived from Homer (cf. *e. g.* Leaf, on *Iliad*, VIII, v. 19); if so, this would be the earliest analogical interpretation of the Homeric *seira* which is attested; cf. below, n. 20. The explanation of the nature of the sun is that of Anaxagoras, as the scholia recall (*Scholia in Euripidem*, ed. E. Schwartz, I [1887], 193 f.), and he may have agreed with the allegorization of the Heracliteans. For Anaxagoras' interest in Homer, cf. F. Wehrli, *Zur Geschichte der allegorischen Deutung Homers im Altertum*, Diss. Basel (1928), 66; 84 f.

the phenomena in place. The student of the Platonic dialogues cannot fail to remember, in addition, that the sun is the offspring of the idea of the Good, the strongest of all bonds, and its analogue in the visible world (*Republic*, 508 b-c).[9] If the movement of the sun is tied up, then the appointed order of the world will be disturbed, just as Zeus threatens to pull all the gods up to heaven, along with the earth and the sea, and to bind the rope around Olympus, so that all things would be hanging in the air (vv. 23–26).

Both the physical and the metaphysical aspects of the Platonic explication were broadened by succeeding generations, and in some instances were merged again to such an extent that it is not always possible to distinguish them clearly. As for that interpretation in which the physical component predominates, some people continued to see in the golden rope an allegory of the sun (*Scholia A, ad* v. 19), or of its rays and the days (Palaephatus, *De incredibilibus*, XVIII; cf. Ps. Lucian, *De astrologia*, 22). The rope symbolized the chain of days of the Aeon, binding together the days of mankind up to that one on which everything will be destroyed, except god himself (Eusthatius, p. 695). Others held that the rope points to the orbits of the stars, which all great naturalists define as firebrands (Heraclitus, *Quaestiones Homericae*, ch. 36).[10] More particularly, it was taken to mean the orbits of the planets and their arrangement on the heaven (Eusthatius, p. 695, 10). Besides, the whole incident related by Homer was now exploited for its allegorical meaning. Zeus' boasting of what he might do to gods, earth, and sea (vv. 23–26) proved that in the poet's view the all-surrounding heaven could

---

[9] F. Boll, *Die Sonne im Glauben und in der Weltanschauung der alten Völker* (1922), 21. He seems the only one to stress this implication of the allegory within the context of the Platonic work.

[10] Heraclitus' book was probably composed in the first century A. D.; it is in the main indebted to Stoic sources.

justly be called the upper part of the spherical cosmos and the region of the earth the part below (Ps. Plutarch, *De vita et poesi Homeri*, ch. 94).[11] Zeus' threat to throw the rebellious gods down into Tartarus, as far below as heaven is high above earth (v. 16), indicated the central position of the earth (Heraclitus, *Quaestiones Homericae*, ch. 36). If Anatolius, the Peripatetic of the third century A.D., is to be trusted, already the "Pythagoreans" found this dogma confirmed by Zeus' words.[12] Finally, the metaphor of the rope was interpreted by the Stoics in two different ways. The rope could be a simile of the "chainlike intertwining," the interlacing of the elements whose nature was to be changed in the end through the general conflagration of the world (Eusthatius, p. 695). Or the rope signified the sun drying up the sea by which it is nourished; eventually, the sun will annihilate even the earth, and thus all that was below will be drawn above into "the heart" of the cosmos; Zeus alone, the personification of the ether, will not be absorbed into it (Eusthatius, p. 695, 10).[13] To put it differently, the altercations between the Olympians, properly understood, yielded the cosmology and cosmography of Homer.

[11] This work shows an eclectic-Pythagorean tendency; its date can perhaps be set at the beginning of the Roman Empire, cf. Wehrli, *op. cit.*, 21; 39.

[12] H. Diels-W. Kranz, *Die Fragmente der Vorsokratiker*, I[5] (1934), p. 225, 18 ff. (28A44). Aristarchus deleted the line (cf. K. Lehrs, *De Aristarchi Studiis Homericis*[2] [1865], 174), while Crates defended it (cf. H. J. Mette, *Sphairopoiia* [1936]. Fr. 39 b).

[13] Lucretius (II, 1153 f.) denies that men descended from heaven by the golden rope, and as Professor Louis A. MacKay, reminds me, the poet is usually understood to refer to a Stoic allegorization of the golden rope mentioned in *Iliad*, VIII. Moreover, Themistius (*Orat.* 32, 363d) is said to prove that the passage "was used in the way hinted at by Lucretius" (Lucretius, ed. H. A. J. Munro, I[3] [1873], *ad. loc.*). Yet, although Themistius speaks of a σειρά of eternal birth, the adjective ἄρρηκτος seems to make certain that what he has in mind is the δεσμὸς ἄρρηκτος with which Zeus fastened the hands of Hera (*Iliad*, XV, 19 f.). This bond actually was interpreted by the Stoics as the unbreakable unity of the elements (Ps. Heraclitus, ch. LX *finis*) that

On the other hand, the metaphysical side of the argument comes to the fore in a statement of Aristotle. Those who believe the origin of motion to be outside of motion, he says, should find appropriate Zeus' assertion (vv. 20–22) that the gods would be unable to overcome him and to drag him down from heaven to earth, even if they tried to do so with all their strength (*Movement of Animals*, 699 b 35 ff.) .[14] And Theophrastus expresses a similar thought, claiming that the prime mover can be expected to be even stronger than the Homeric Zeus who boasts (v. 24) that he can do what his fellow gods are unable to accomplish (*Metaphysics*, II, 9, 5b15–17). While Aristotle and Theophrastus avail themselves of Homer's verses to illustrate the position of the transcendental prime mover, others were more realistic and thought that the poet in Zeus' menacing speech enigmatically suggested the merit of monarchy, for the rule of the many would be even worse in heaven than on earth (Eusthatius, p. 695, 10; *Scholia A, ad* vv. 25–26) . Moreover, this Zeus, the Stoics claimed, is the personification of fate that holds sway over heaven and earth (v. 27; Eusthatius, p. 695) . Homer, like all great philosophers, acknowledged one supreme deity. Does not Zeus end his warnings (v. 27) by affirming his superiority over men and gods alike? Does not Athena humbly answer the father of all, the supreme of lords (v. 31) ? Does she not concede (v. 32) : " We know only too well that your might

create animals and men (*ibid., init.*). The whole description of Hera's punishment through Zeus (XV, 18-21) symbolized the genesis of the cosmos (cf. J. Stern, *Homerstudien der Stoiker* [1893], 16). I should therefore suggest that Lucretius too was thinking of an interpretation of *Iliad*, XV rather than of *Iliad*, VIII (for *superne . . . de caelo*, cf. ὑψόθεν [XV, 18] and Ps. Heraclitus on this word) .

[14] The genuineness of this treatise has been proved by W. Jaeger, *Hermes*, 48 (1913) , 33, who has also pointed out that the use of the Homeric verses here agrees with Aristotle's general attitude as expressed in Book XII of the *Metaphysics*.

is dauntless " (Ps. Plutarch, *De vita et poesi Homeri*, 114) ?
Thus, he who challenged his peers to a tug of war emerged as
the highest deity, an understanding of the Homeric account
that apparently was quite commonly accepted. Lucian, in his
Menippean dialogues, repeatedly pokes fun at the golden chain
of Zeus and his pretense at being omnipotent, whereas Christian Apologists of approximately the same time concluded from
the same evidence that Homer agreed with their own mono-
theistic teaching.[15]

From the testimony adduced it is clear, I think, that when
the Middle Platonists expressed their concept of the structure
of the universe through the metaphor of the golden chain, they
merely followed an old-established procedure. At that time, the
episode at the beginning of the Eighth Book of the *Iliad* had
long been of central importance for philosophical allegorizers.
To the modern reader, the Homeric tale has alternately appeared
as a burlesque mockery of the divine, or as a poetical description
of the gods' character that is imbued with tragic grandeur.[16]
To the ancients, at least to those who wished to extract Homer's
philosophy in agreement with their own predilections, it was
fraught with deep meaning, a clue to Homer's physical and
metaphysical beliefs. How this came about, it is difficult to
determine. The love of etymologies may have provided the
starting point for speculation. The rope, the *seira*, may have

[15] For Lucian, cf. e. g. *Juppiter confutatus*, 4; other passages have been
collected by R. Helm, *Lucian und Menipp* (1906), 137. Even the *Scholia A*,
ad vv. 25-26 raise the question, how Zeus can be the strongest, if once he was
overcome by others (*Iliad*, I, 400). On the other hand, Vettius Valens,
Anthologiae, IX, 8, p. 347, 7 ff. Kroll, sees in lines 19 ff. proof of Zeus' self-
restraint and willingness not to overstep the law; this " mystic " interpretation
unfortunately is mutilated by a lacuna. For the Christian view, cf. Ps.
Justinus, *Cohortatio ad Graecos*, 24 (*Patrologia Graeca*, VI, p. 284 Migne).

[16] Cf. e. g. W. Nestle, *Anfänge einer Götterburleske bei Homer*, in *Griechische Studien* (1948), 14.

been brought together with the star, *Seirios*, or with Zeus *Seiren*, of whom the poet, Antimachus, affirms that he was named after *Sirius*, the dog-star rising in the month of the greatest summer heat.[17] Orphic poets referred to a golden rope which Zeus, "in accordance with the laws laid down by the goddess, Night, winds around all things." It is not certain that this statement formed part of the early Orphic doctrine, and consequently one cannot be sure that it helped in instigating the preoccupation of philosophers with the golden rope of Homer. But at one moment or other it must have provided at least an additional reason for the interest in the Homeric scene.

In the third century B. C., at any rate, the question could be asked, whether the Orphic rope may not be identical with that of Homer, for, as Philodemus attests, Cleanthes and Chrysippus tried to reconcile their own views with those of Homer and Orpheus and Musaeus.[18] Decisive perhaps was the fact that Zeus' threat to pull up earth, sea, and gods is indeed rather puzzling,

---

[17] M. Wohlrab, *Platonis Opera*, III²,1 (1891), commenting on the *Theaetetus* passage, where the golden *seira* is identified with the sun, quotes a gloss of Suidas: σειρ, σειρός: ὁ ἥλιος; cf. also O. Apelt's note in his translation, *Platons Dialog Theätet*⁴ (1923), 161. For Antimachus, cf. B. Wyss, *Antimachi Colophonii Reliquiae* (1936), Fr. 31. Wyss interprets: *Juppiter torrens*; cf. A. B. Cook, *Zeus*, I (1914), 740. For the rôle which etymologies played in early interpretations, cf. the Platonic *Cratylus*, and in general Wehrli, *op. cit.*, 85 ff., who has also drawn attention to the fact that the allegorization of the golden chain is the oldest philosophical allegorization of a Homeric concept that has survived (88). Whether or not an ethical interpretation preceded the philosophical one, in this instance as perhaps in all others, I am not prepared to decide.

[18] For the Orphic references to a golden chain, cf. O. Kern, *Orphicorum Fragmenta* (1922), Fr. 166; for Cleanthes and Chrysippus, cf. I, 539 Arnim. W. Nestle, *Vom Mythos zum Logos* (1942), 129, apparently considers Fr. 166 part of the old Orphic theogony; he is even inclined to trace the beginning of all allegorization of Homer to the Orphics. But the only fact that can be established is that the goddess, Night, was regarded as the supreme deity in the older stratum of the Orphic tradition; cf. Fr. 28 Kern (Eudemus) and I. M. Linforth, *The Arts of Orpheus* (1941), 154 f.

and that hardly any other passage in the *Iliad* sketches so briefly and succinctly a scheme of the whole world. Zeus' words about Tartarus and its precise location in regard to Hades, as well as in regard to the distance between heaven and earth (v. 16), are spoken in the manner of a philosopher, as a late commentator remarks (Eusthatius, p. 694, 40); they recall an almost identical assertion in Hesiod's *Theogony* (v. 720). And surely, no scene in Homer gives a more vivid and unmistakable impression of the true distribution of power among the Olympians.[19]

Whatever the adequate cause of the allegorization, the Middle Platonists only did what all the philosophers on whose systems they based their own doctrine—Plato, Aristotle, the Stoics—had done before them. Moreover, allowing for certain changes made necessary by their own peculiar theories, their reading of the time-hallowed cipher was but the almost logical consequence of earlier interpretations. The theology that Aristides expounds in his speech *On Zeus* presupposes the dogma of Zeus' predominance; it takes it for granted that the golden rope has some cosmic significance. But Zeus is now regarded not only as a deity, incorporeal and comprehensible by reason alone (Ps. Plutarch, *De vita et poesi Homeri*, 114), or as fate (Eusthatius, p. 695); he is thought of as a personal god, as the creator of the world over which he rules, the one who unifies the diversity of being. Thus, while according to Homer Zeus is able, if he feels it necessary or if he so wishes, to pull up by a rope to his heavenly abode gods and sea and earth, according to Aristides he holds forever all things that he has created; in the manner of Homer's chain they are fastened upon and suspended from

---

[19] The similarity between *Iliad*, VIII, 16 and Hesiod, *Theogony*, 720, was noted by K. Amcis-C. Hentze, *Homers Ilias*, I⁴ (1894), *ad loc.* Linguistic peculiarities of the lines and Hesiodic parallels are discussed by R. Mackrodt, *Der Olymp in Ilias und Odyssee*, Programm Eisenberg (1882), 9 f.

him. The epic picture of what might happen under certain circumstances is transformed—as is fitting for a symbol—into a description of what does happen from eternity to eternity. The rope is taken to mean a chain, the links of which are made up of the various parts of the cosmos connected and held together by Zeus.[20]

Moreover, this chain of Zeus Aristides finds worthy of praise in preference to "that golden chain or any other chain one might imagine." The binding power of Necessity, or Eros and Aphrodite had played a primary part in early cosmological theories; Necessity as the "concatenation of causes" and the golden chain of Aphrodite were familiar expressions in Aristides' time.[21] Yet these chains symbolized a force that works from without, that coerces matter into a unity alien to itself. Aristides subordinates them to Zeus. Eros and Ananke, he continues immediately following his pronouncement on Zeus, are themselves children of the king of gods, begotten by him at the beginning

[20] My interpretation of Aristides' understanding of the Homeric description presupposes that he did not read vv. 25-26, according to which Zeus intends to bind the rope around Olympus, so that all things will be hanging in the air. These lines were deleted by Zenodotus, because they seemed to contradict a statement previously made by Homer about Mount Olympus; cf. Lehrs, *op. cit.*, 168. They are also omitted in another speech of Aristides (28, Par. 45 Keil), where he quotes *Iliad*, VIII, 17-27. *Scholia A, ad* vv. 25-26, however, give the impression that it was just these lines which were taken to mean that everything is dependent on god. The Middle Platonic commentary on the *Theaetetus, Berliner Klassikertexte*, II (1905), 49, explains only Plato's statement on the golden rope and does not help to clarify Aristides' views. I should note that Aristides paraphrases σειρά by ἅλυσις; to him, then, as to all later philosophers, the "rope" definitely was a "chain." Whether or not the two terms were used interchangeably before him, cannot be ascertained. Some of the Stoic allegorizations (cf. above p. 52) seem to indicate such a usage, especially the identification of the rope with Fate.

[21] For Aristides' polemic against older cosmogonies, cf. Amann, *op. cit.*, 76 ff. The chain of Aphrodite is mentioned *e. g.* by Lucian, *Demosthenis Encomium*, 13. For Fate as the concatenation of causes, cf. *St. V. Fr.*, II, 917 Arnim, and Ps. Plutarch, *De fato*, 570 b; also 574 c: ὁ τῆς ἁλύσεως λόγος.

of the world "so that they should bind the universe together for him" (*In Jovem*, 15). In this way, the work of Eros and Ananke becomes an effluence of Zeus' own power. Their chains, as well as that of Zeus himself, are taken to symbolize a unity that resides within, for all creation is itself part of the creator to whom it owes its existence.

Thus the *aurea catena Homeri* was established by the Middle Platonists as a figurative expression of the Scale of Being. A poetical phrase became a philosophical catchword; the implement of an athletic contest became a metaphor of the innermost essence of the universe. Could it be that behind Homer's own fancy a symbol was hidden which he playfully transformed, and that later philosophers in their attempts to find an allegorical meaning in his story only reverted to its original significance? The romanticists among the nineteenth century writers on mythology were prone to call the golden chain a mythical or religious *Ursymbol*, clearly expressed in Hindu sacred literature by Vishnu, who speaks of the cosmos as suspended from himself "like a row of pearls on a string." Such an opinion will nowadays hardly be acceptable to anyone.[22] Nor does the more recent interpretation of the chain as an astronomical *Ursymbol* seem any more satisfactory. In the view of certain peoples, the Milky Way was thought to be an immense rope, and the golden rope hung from heaven, it has therefore been said, may have been suggested to Homer by a popular conception of the galaxy. But no remnant of such a belief on the part of the Greeks has survived, and what may be true of other times and other countries need not necessarily be true of them.[23]

[22] F. Creuzer, *Symbolik und Mythologie der alten Völker*, I (1810), 116 ff., quoting from Fr. Schlegel, *Über die Sprache und Weisheit der Inder*, 303.

[23] The astronomical interpretation has been proposed by A. B. Cook, *Zeus*, II, 2 (1925), 1211, with reference to W. Gundel, *Sterne und Sternbilder im Glauben des Altertums und der Neuzeit* (1922), 46. Concerning the Milky

In Greek popular tradition the rope is of some importance. In the fantasy of the people it is connected with the figure of death. It occurs in magic beliefs and rituals. Binding by a rope is a means of sorcery. Closely related to such ideas is the simile of the thread of life which the Fates spin on their distaff, and which in Germanic mythology reappears as the rope of Fate. These views apparently were widely current. Even Homer takes notice of some of them. He frequently speaks of the thread of life. Once, the gods attempted to bind their king and father (*Iliad*, I, 400), a fact that ancient interpreters found it hard to reconcile with the strength of Zeus, as it is pictured in the Eighth Book of the *Iliad* (*Scholia A, ad* vv. 25–26). Zeus himself fastened around Hera's hands a golden bond "that might not be broken" (*Iliad*, XV, vv. 19–20). That he threatens to fasten the golden rope around Olympus and thus to hold earth and sea in mid air, could be another reminiscence of such popular beliefs in the power of the rope. Still, in this way one may explain a detail of the story, but it can scarcely be the explanation of the whole tale.[24]

Among the divine figures it seems that Hecate, and she alone,

---

Way as a rope in Babylonian mythology, cf. R. Eisler, *Weltenmantel und Himmelszelt*, I (1910), 98. The philosophical use of such a simile, as for instance in the myth of the Platonic *Republic* (616 b-c), is of course quite a different matter.

[24] The testimony on Greek popular beliefs has been collected by J. Heckenbach, *De nuditate sacra sacrisque vinculis, R. G. V. V.*, XI, 3 (1911), esp. 87 ff., and J. Scheftelowitz, *Das Schlingen- und Netzmotiv im Glauben und Brauch der Völker, R. G. V. V.*, XII (1912-13), Heft 2, *passim*. For folktales in Homer, cf. G. M. Calhoun, Homer's Gods, *T. A. P. A.*, LXVIII (1937), 17, and *A. J. P.*, LVIII (1937), 267. For the thread of life in Homer, cf. *Iliad*, XX, 128; XXIV, 210; *Odyssey*, VII, 198. The reference to the rope of Fate in Germanic mythology I found in J. J. Bachofen, *Versuch über die Gräbersymbolik der Alten*[2] (1925), 315; cf. W. Mannhardt, *Germanische Mythen* (1858). Bachofen interprets the rope of Ocnus, the plaiter, as the rope of life; even if this interpretation were correct, it would not help to explain Homer, since the story seems to be of much later origin.

appears on late monuments with a key and a rope as her attributes. They are commonly understood to be identical in meaning and to indicate her power to open and close the gates of Hades, the rope being the older means by which to fasten a door. But originally, Hecate was not a goddess of the nether world. She was one of the great mother goddesses, one of the most highly revered deities of Asia Minor. Hesiod's *Theogony* describes her might, the privileges granted to her by Zeus "in earth and in heaven and in sea" (v. 427).[25] Homer never mentions Hecate. She belongs to a world that was superseded by the Olympian religion and mythology. Could the rope have been an ancient attribute of Hecate, who was sovereign over the three realms of the cosmos, signifying her all-pervading power? Could Homer have thought of this attribute when he let Zeus challenge his peers to a rope-pulling contest in which the king of gods threatens to pull up gods and earth and sea? Did he smile deprecatingly at another, a defeated mythology? Or does Homer's account betray the faint memory of a fight between some opposing powers? In Germanic mythology, Thor, the god of thunder and lightning, is said to have pulled up by a chain the Midgard serpent, a monster that surrounded the whole earth. The similarity of the Homeric account and the Nordic saga does not suffice to assume a common source of the two, or to aver that there must have been a deeper significance behind the Homeric tale. But the parallel is striking, and it

[25] The Hecate monuments are surveyed by E. Petersen, *Die dreigestaltige Hekate, Archaeol.-epigraph. Mitt. aus Oesterreich*, IV (1880), 140-74; V (1881), 1-84, esp. 80; cf. also W. H. Roscher, *Lexikon der griech. u. röm. Mythologie, s.v. Hekate*, I, 2 (1886-90), *col.* 1906. For key and rope, cf. Eusthatius, *In Odysseam*, p. 1923, 50, For Hecate and her original power, cf. O. Kern, *Die Religion der Griechen*, I (1926), 45 ff., who has also shown, *op. cit.*, 245 ff., that one cannot eliminate the hymn on Hecate as an "Orphic" interpolation and that the lines form an intrinsic part of the *Theogony*.

emphasizes the possibility that Homer may not merely have given free rein to his fantasy.[26]

Which one of these speculations comes nearest to the truth, or whether it is legitimate at all to ask if the Homeric story originally had a symbolic meaning, will probably never be known for certain. To the Greeks, at any rate, Zeus' warnings addressed to the assembled gods and goddesses revealed nothing more than the thought of Homer. The Middle Platonists, like all earlier philosophers, turned to Homer not as a writer of hieratic poetry, but as the father of philosophy, whose ideas, expressed in mythological language, needed and demanded translation into rational concepts.

Once they had found in the chain a metaphor of the Scale of Being, one would almost expect Plotinus to have adopted the simile for his intellectual vision of the One and the Many and their interrelation. He himself is inclined to speak, in terms similar to those used by Aristotle and by the Middle Platonists, of things as fastened upon the Good (*e. g. Enneads*, V, 5, 9); in the same context he refers to a hand grasping the universe at its extremity (VI, 4, 7). Yet his favorite illustrations of the process of emanation are heat emanating from fire, cold originating from snow, rays sent forth by the sun, light reflected by a mirror, a stream that issues from its source, sap that ascends from the root. In other words, Plotinus usually selects physical or biological processes for his comparisons. His highest transcendent being is above will and intellect, as it is above the activity of the demiurge. Besides, his allegorizations are few and cautious. He pays scant attention to the gods of mythology.[27]

[26] The comparison between the episode in Homer and the Thor story has been made by L. Radermacher, *Mythos und Sage bei den Griechen* (1938), 110. I should mention that Kern, *op. cit.*, 202; 209, considers the Homeric lines a remnant of hieratic poetry.

[27] Cf. *Enneads*, V, 4, 1, and E. Bréhier, *Plotin, Ennéades*, V (1931), *ad*

Who then introduced the metaphor of the chain into Neo-Platonism and transmitted it to Macrobius? Porphyry and Iamblichus are the two philosophers to whom Macrobius is indebted for his understanding of the Plotinian teaching, and Porphyry has been suggested as the one to whom he may owe the concept of the *aurea catena Homeri*.[28] However, reflecting on the general attitude of Porphyry one wonders whether this disciple of the master could really have added the metaphor in question. Much as he was given to allegorizations of Homer and to a belief in the traditional religion before he became a Neo-Platonist, after his conversion he closely followed in the footsteps of Plotinus; he interpreted religion and mythology in an ethical, rather than in a metaphysical sense. With Iamblichus, a change set in. The value of the religious inheritance was reaffirmed. Allegorization was now extended to be all-inclusive, it became systematic and was concerned with the transcendental significance of religion. The will of the gods, their power, was strongly emphasized. Within the context of such an interpretation of the world, the chain of Zeus, who possesses all the qualities which he creates, seems to have its proper place, and it therefore appears likely that Iamblichus or one of his followers, rather than Porphyry, was the source of Macrobius.[29]

loc.; also Witt, *op. cit.*, 135, whose formulation I have followed. E. Zeller, *Die Philosophie der Griechen*[3], III, 2 (1881), 499, note 2, has noted the agreement between Plotinus and Aristotle. For Plotinus' concept of the highest being, cf. Zeller, *op. cit.*, III, 2, p. 496; for his attitude toward mythology, cf. C. H. Kirchner, *Die Philosophie des Plotin* (1854), 190 ff.

[28] Cf. Schedler, *op. cit.*, 12. For Macrobius' sources in general, cf. Ueberweg-Praechter, *op. cit.*, 651 f.

[29] For Porphyry, cf. J. Bidez, *Vie de Porphyre* (1913); his method of allegorization, esp. 108 f. For Iamblichus and his position, cf. K. Praechter, *Genethliakon für C. Robert* (1910), 128 ff.; Ueberweg-Praechter, *op. cit.*, 615 f. The contrast between the two leading Neo-Platonists has recently been accentuated by N. H. Baynes, *The Hellenistic Civilization and East Rome* (The James Bryce Memorial Lecture, 1946), 27 f.

One other fact should be noted. Among the later Neo-Platonists—all of them deeply influenced by the teaching of the "divine Iamblichus"—Proclus is the first to have glorified the golden chain of Homer as a cosmic symbol. He identifies it with the golden chain of Orpheus and with the Platonic *desmos*, "the fairest of all bonds." The concept of the chain, or series, is basic for his whole explanation of the universe.[30] But he also speaks of chains linking men to specific gods, their patrons or patronymic deities, as it were, and taken in this sense, the metaphor of the chain is part and parcel of its usage as a figurative expression of the Scale of Being. Now, the chain symbol of spiritual lineage can be traced to earlier writers, to the generation preceding Macrobius or contemporary with him. Thus, to Eunapius, Julian's claim to being descended from the sun is not comparable to Olympia's assertion that her son, Alexander, was the offspring of Zeus; Julian's statement rather implies the belief that he was bound to the solar kingdom by a "golden chain," in the same way in which the Platonic Socrates affirms: we are the followers of Zeus; others are the followers of other gods.[31] The theoretical exegesis is derived from Plato, as Eunapius himself states; the language in which it is couched is not. In the passage of the *Phaedrus* (250 b) to which Eunapius refers, Plato does not speak of a chain. Even in the *Ion*, where poets and

[30] Concerning the golden chain of Homer, cf. especially Proclus, *In Timaeum*, 28 c (I, p. 314, 17 ff. Diehl); also Fr. 166 Kern (cf. above, note 18). For σειρά in a general sense, cf. *e. g. The Elements of Theology*, ed. E. R. Dodds (1933), *Propositio* 21, and Dodds' note *ad loc*. The hymns of Proclus provide numerous instances of the chain connecting gods and men. After Proclus, Damascius, *Dubitationes et Solutiones*, ed. C. A. Ruelle, I (1889), esp. 154, is most explicit about the meaning of the chain.

[31] Cf. *Fragmenta Historicorum Graecorum*, ed. C. Müller, IV (1868), 24 (Fr. 24). The passage is referred to by F. Creuzer, *Plotini Opera Omnia*, III (1835), 323, *ad Enn.* VI, 1, 3. Eunapius uses the simile of the chain also in his *Vita Porphyrii*, 457 Boissonade.

rhapsodes are said to be suspended from the Muses, while from them a cluster or chain " of other persons is suspended to take over the inspiration " (533 e), he bases his simile not on the example of the chain, but on that of the magnet and the iron rings which it attracts. Obviously, then, Eunapius, the historian of the school of Iamblichus, has replaced the terminology of Plato by that of Homer. For him, the Homeric chain must have been an established symbol of the connection between god and man, between the divine and part of the cosmos.[32] The same figure of speech repeatedly occurs in the hymns of Synesius, another follower of Iamblichus and a contemporary of Macrobius. This, I think, is additional reason to hold that it was Iamblichus, or the circle around him, who considered the chain a figurative expression applicable to Plotinus' theory of the Scale of Being; in other instances, too, they were not averse to accepting pre-Plotinian concepts.[33]

[32] In this context it is interesting to recall that Lucian, whose writings Eunapius must have known quite well (*Vita Sophistorum, Prooemium,* 454 Boissonade), describes a statue of the Celtic Heracles, the god of eloquence, from whose tongue chains of gold and amber are suspended, by which in turn the god's worshippers are fettered (*Hercules,* 3; cf. F. Koepp, *Ognios,* in *Bonner Jahrbücher,* Heft 125 [1919], 38 ff.). Whether or not such a statue actually existed, the description, which was to have great influence on Renaissance art, certainly agrees with Lucian's own views, for he says that the teacher " lets down his words, just as the Homeric Zeus lets down his golden chain," thus pulling up his pupils (*Hermotimus,* 3); he applies the picture of the chain also to his own speech (*Hercules,* 8). Lucian, then, sees in the chain a simile of inspiration through oratory, and such a figure of speech may be a contamination of the Homeric language with the theory of the *Ion*—a similar contamination occurs in alchemistic literature, where the " Platonic rings " and the " Homeric chain " are used interchangeably; cf. F. Hoefer, *Histoire de la chimie,* II (1866) 245 f.; H. Kopp, *Aurea Catena Homeri* (1880). On the other hand, Eusthatius, p. 695, 60, maintains that the golden chain and the whole passage in which it occurs formed a *topos* for the encomiastic literature on kingship. Even if Eunapius knew of such a rhetorical theory, he transformed it into a philosophical doctrine.

[33] Wilamowitz, *Sitzungsber. Berlin Akad.* (1907), 272 ff., has shown that,

Through the works of Macrobius and Proclus above all, the metaphor of the chain then came to be a phrase typical of Neo-Platonic teaching. Later generations forgot that the *aurea catena Homeri* had been interpreted and reinterpreted by writers preceding the Neo-Platonists, that in fact it had been a concept highly important in all Greek philosophy and literature, just as, in Professor Lovejoy's words, it was to be "one of the most famous in the vocabulary of Occidental philosophy, science, and reflective poetry." [34]

before Proclus, the chain as a symbol of human descent occurs in Synesius. As the ultimate source of the simile he names Homer and Orpheus (cf. also Dodds, *op .cit.*, 208 f.) , and he points out the necessity of determining the intermediate steps in the history of the metaphor. For other examples of a "harking back to pre-Plotinian sources . . . in later Neo-Platonism," cf. Dodds, *op. cit.*, 258.

[34] *The Great Chain of Being*, p. vii. Cf. now also E. Wolff, *Die goldene Kette* (Die Aurea Catena Homeri in der englischen Literatur von Chaucer bis Wordsworth) [1947].

LEO SPITZER

Language—The Basis of Science, Philosophy and Poetry

The majority of men behave toward language as our primitive ancestors did toward their wives: they gladly accepted their service, their ever-abiding presence, the atmosphere they gave to their lives, but scarcely thought or spoke about them—unless they found them unfaithful, unless Eve betrayed her husband. The rôle of language as betrayer has recently forced itself into undue prominence, thanks to the so-called school of semanticists. But language as such, whether it serves or betrays, is loved perhaps only by a few, the poets and the philologists. Poets tend rather to be too much in love with language to be able to speak rationally about it—a capacity given only to the philologists who combine, with their love for language from which their name derives, the calm of the scholar who is able to define what he loves (and it is just such a definition which will be attempted in this essay).

The famous French philologist Gaston Paris once wrote to a friend: " J'ai la philologie calme: c'est pour moi une épouse, non pas une amante." And yet for all their calm, most philologists find it difficult to understand why *all* scholars have not become philologists, since the first scientific tool in all fields of learning is language: chronologically first and first in importance.

For every scientific statement is couched in language; even an algebraic equation such as $x = a^2 + b^2$ is a sentence, grammatically construed according to the prevailing structure of Indo-European sentences, containing a subject and a predicate, together with the additional feature, not required in all those languages, of a copula. And the words of this sentence have a premathematical history which reveals their origin in the common speech of those peoples who have been concerned with the development of mathematics: for instance, the symbol x goes back to the initial consonant of the Arabic word for ' thing,' *šay*, that is, to the sibilant *š*, which was written x in Old Spanish by both Christians and Arabs (cf. the French pronunciation *Don Quichotte* for what is written in English *Don Quixote*). Again, *square* said of a number, testifies to a word-usage of the Pythagoreans, who used the corresponding Greek term ' *tetragone* ' not only for the geometrical figure, but also for the arithmetical product of a number multiplied by itself, because they saw numbers geometrically arranged, in our case the a^2 as the area of a geometrical square with equal sides of the length a. The algebraic symbols a, b, and x have been added to the common language in order to designate relational, not numeric values, classified into knowns and unknowns; the equal sign as a new type of copula freed from grammatical flection; the plus sign as a new type of conjunction opposed to the minus sign; and the whole mathematical nomenclature, detached as it is from any particular spoken national language, has the advantage of representing a system of internationally valid ideograms perceptible to the eye without the detour via the spoken particular languages. The mathematical terms are thus improvements on the common language—terms which may even find their way back to the common language. The eighteenth century philosopher Condillac has said: "Une science n'est qu'une langue bien faite," and similarly the German essayist Lichtenberg has stated that our whole philosophy amounts to no more than to correction of word-usage.

Now just as the creation of a scientific or philosophical vocabulary represents a refinement on common speech, so our everyday spoken language is itself the result of innumerable refinements and creations, wrought by the human mind in the desire better to orientate itself in the labyrinth of the world—a tremendous improvement over the speechless state of the animals, indeed the greatest scientific progress before science in our sense was invented. We may define the spoken language as a system of sounds and sound-groups, produced by the delicate minimum movements of our articulatory apparatus, which are made to symbolize thoughts that have crystallized around certain points: out of the incessant and turbid flow of life certain entities have been isolated and endowed with a relative acoustic fixity and duration with the result that predications about them can be made. Without acoustic fixations by words of concepts such as *night* and *day, atom, electricity,* acoustic fixations which can in turn be fixed in writing, the human individual would have to recapitulate for every new thought the whole bulk of thoughts of mankind on the subject. As Shelley says: language "rules a throng of thought and forms which else senseless and shapeless were."

Now such linguistic fixations, or words, as they are offered to the individual speaker of a language, are *to him* arbitrary, conventional, imposed by the chance of his being born into a particular speaking community. In general, no motivation of the meaning of a particular sound group or word can be given by the speaker: in the terms of Plato, no motivation for the words can be given by the nature (φύσει) of the things designated.

Why does *horse* not mean *cat* or the reverse? Why is the horse called in Italian *cavallo* and in German *Pferd*? And even in the case of onomatopoeias and interjections where an acoustic motivation of the words is possible, the particular speaker is bound to respect the convention of his speaking community: the rooster crows *cockadoodledoo* in English, *cocorico* in French, *kikeriki* in German, and still differently in other languages; if someone steps on your foot you will cry *ouch!* if you are an American, *au!* if German, *aïe!* if French. Nevertheless, the single speaker who uses *cavallo* in Italian, *Pferd* in German, *horse* in English can expect to be understood, or understood fairly well, by his fellow-countrymen as if in consequence of a tacit convention or pact—θέσει, as Plato called it. It is this unwritten, but daily-renewed linguistic contract with one's co-citizens, that daily plebiscite, which makes national cohesion possible—as is illustrated in reverse by the Biblical story of the confusion of tongues at the tower of Babel. The average member of a speaking community feels so well at home in his mother-tongue that he would naively boast that *no other* language can express outward reality better than his: the anecdote of a Tyrolian German discussing with a Tyrolian Italian the merits of their respective languages is well-known. The German brings the discussion to a close with the remark: " You call a ' Pferd ' a ' cavallo ' but it *is* a ' Pferd.' "

I have said that speakers of the same language understand each other *fairly* well, for in most cases the understanding is indeed not complete within the same community: cases of absolute unambiguity as the two mathematical usages of the term *square* are rather rare and represent the maximum possibility of understanding through words. With the majority of the words no such unanimity of understanding exists: the noun *square* itself has in the common language four or five different senses. In order to know what the word actually means in a certain situation we must know the context; if the context is zero, as happens to be the rule in newspaper headlines, we often fail to reach certainty. But even when the context is given, all the speakers do not always mean exactly the same when using a particular word: *democracy* is different according to the Communist and the non-Communist creed; and surely not all speakers are agreed on what shade of color is *red* as opposed to *pink*.

Understanding is then only based on that semantic kernel of the words on which all speakers of a language are agreed, while the semantic fringes are blurred. The founder of modern philosophy of language, Wilhelm von Humboldt, was right in saying that the speaking individual does not offer to his fellow speaker objective signs for the things expressed, nor does he compel him by his verbal utterance to represent to himself exactly the same thing as that meant by him, but is satisfied with, as it were, pressing down the homologous *key* of the other's respective mental keyboard, with establishing only the same link in the chain of associations of things with words, so that there are elicited corresponding, though not exactly identical, responses.

Yet irrespective of the variable ratio of understanding our words may find, we behave generally naively as though we were perfectly understood. And this illusion is one of the great sources of man's happiness: it gives him the feeling of being surrounded by a friendly world which shares with him all the associations he may have built up in his lifetime—for man fears nothing more than isolation in the universe. It is the enjoyment of the community of language which works at all public gatherings wherein the individual communes with the collective spirit. Great actors or orators give us a feeling of strength and elation because we realize that the maximum of expressivity with which they are able to endow the common language does not disrupt the flow of understanding between them and us. And even in our most personal and intimate reactions we welcome the social character of the word that expresses *us* in terms of age-old experiences of the community: when we feel tender or sad we are likely to say to ourselves the words *tender* or *sad* and feel even tenderer or sadder—because we somehow have received a ratification, by the language of the community, of our personal state of mind. It is also their quality of social reassurance that keeps adages, " old saws," alive.

Language is then a system of arbitrary, conventional, ambiguous signs generally not felt as ambiguous, and, in addition, a system in movement at which the community is constantly working. The use of the language by the community brings about change—changes mainly due to shifts of attention which in turn are conditioned by the law of diminishing returns, by the fact that experiences which have become familiar to us no longer interest us. We may assume, for example, that for primitive man every situation was unique and required a unique expression, a new kind of interjection or proper name, but that with his growing experience he became able to subsume a new situation under an older one and to express the former as a variant of the latter: his attention shifted from the unique to the regular, from the proper name to the common noun stage: Latin *tatta* and *mamma* are originally exclamations of the babbling child, reserved for the father and the mother, *proper names* characterizing these unique persons in the family; but the common nouns *pater - mater,* offering the babbling syllables *pă-mā-* and provided with the suffix *-ter,* testify already to a classification, the suffix being the linguistic expression of a regularity perceived in the world, indeed a rhyme symbolizing a perceived analogy by equality of sound.

The most frequent suffixes are found in the paradigms of nouns and verbs; in primitive times the verbal expressions *I go* and *we go* may have appeared as quite different experiences, not as concrete variants of the abstract verb *to go*: a remainder of such primitive thinking is the Romance so-called suppletive conjugation: French *je vais - nous allons,* Italian *vo - andiamo,* or the similar opposition in English *I go - I went.* The so-called irregular verbs, generally the ones most frequently used in our languages, are remnants of a state of civilization in which the power of abstraction was not yet sufficiently strong to see, behind the actions of different persons, one common abstract denominator. Regular flexion is a means by which new concrete expressions of actions can be subsumed under one heading. That nearly all third persons singular of the present have an *-s* ending in English is a conquest of the abstracting mind that posits a He-She-It-category. A minimum articulation, that sibilant *-s* formed by a certain position of the tongue against the teeth, has been given the task of symbolizing a grammatical category, that of activity of a third person while the rest of the paradigm of the present is characterized by a zero-ending: *he says—I say, you say.* It would seem that this system, which introduces a classifying principle into activity, a system in itself as neat and as scientific as that of Linnaeus in botany, should stay for ever in English. But, strangely enough, the *-s* as the privilege of the third person is not immune from change: one hears in colloquial renderings of a dialogue such forms as *says she, says I* and even *says you.* What has happened here, is that the attention of the speakers has shifted from the opposition: *-s* for the third person, zero for the other persons, to the relationship between partners in conversation, to the idea of their being united by the conversation: *says he - says I,* with the result that the *-s* of the third person passes to the first and second. Were

this popular innovation to be generalized, winning out over
the objections of the schools and other conservative circles, the
whole conjugational system of English would be wrecked and
replaced by a new system in which the -*s* would be characteristic
of the whole present tense—a change that would be welcomed
by the contemporary "Leave your language alone" school of
grammarians.

But this much must be granted to those linguistic anarchists,
that such changes are not only mistakes or caprices of the
language, but new categorizations due to shift of attention: as
we have learnt from Freud, no mistake is only a mistake; no
single mistake or innovation that becomes generalized in a
language is in itself without meaning—although the sum total
of the mistakes or changes that in the course of history have
been superimposed one upon the other may give us a picture,
reminiscent of the silhouette of European cities that have grown
out of medieval towns, of confusion and irregularity which are
mainly due to the conflict between the innovating and the conservative tendencies, or between several innovations. One may
regret the appearance, in the twentieth century American English
of the show business, of new words such as *motorcade* or *aquacade*
which have been coined with a spurious suffix—*cade* cut out of
the body of the model word *cavalcade*, of French origin. But
not basically different are much older formations in the international lingo of musicians such as *trio* with an -*o* borrowed
from *duo*, the Latin word for 'duet' [and French *quintuor
sextuor septuor octuor* ('quintette, sextette, etc.') are modelled
on the Latin word *quattuor* 'quartette']. In such violent linguistic mutilations, which are characteristic of the restlessness of
the musical guild and the show-business people, there manifests
itself an attitude of dissatisfaction with the traditionally given
words, a shift of attention away from linguistic correctness. But

such an attitude occurs to some degree at *all* periods in language, and not only in the fields of flexion and suffixation.

The wear and tear undergone by language shows itself also in the semantic field. The English adverb *much* is in part replaced by *very*, a more emotional word originally meaning ' truly,' and by expressions involving exaggeration such as *enormously, exceedingly, awfully, devastatingly*. Similarly the Old French adverb *mout* (from Latin *multum*) has been replaced by *beaucoup, force, bien*; in Rhetoromance ' much ' is expressed by *milliarium* ' a thousand,' etc. The language of modern advertising lives on exaggeration, but the law of diminishing returns can also be shown to operate here: after the overuse of superlatives ("the finest car in the world"), a more modest comparative, the comparative without comparison, is discovered ("a better car"—better than what?), and after so many advertisements of 100 per cent purity the claim of Ivory Soap to only $99^{44}/_{100}$th per cent purity, with its novelty of precision in understatement, is a gain in expressivity.

The same drive toward the novel, the expressive exists also in the phonetic development of the language: probably because the speaking communities become tired of the familiar articulations they engage in those sound-shifts of which our historical grammars are full: the *g* of Germanic *garden* develops to the *j* of French *jardin*, a development which must have started with a minimum displacement in the pronunciation of the *g*—comparable to the *g'arden* pronunciation of our Virginians: the alterations *garden* > *g'arden* > *jardin* ultimately root in man's constant urge to make his language more expressive, by an exaggeration of the current pronunciation of sounds which leads to their alteration. The law of the minimum effort is not generally respected in language, which is inclined rather to squander efforts than to economize them. Limits to such expenditure of expressivity are imposed only by the system of the language as a whole; it may happen that the general system checks the particular innovation. In such cases the speaker is faced with the alternative: " Shall I actually say *g'arden, I says, devastatingly,* or shall I cling to the older system of expression? " Perhaps at any moment in the course of the development of any living language a change is taking place, perhaps just beginning, perhaps reaching standardization; a change that may consist in additions to the language or in eliminations from it, as the seventeenth century English linguist Bentley has said: " Every living language, like the perspiring bodies of living creatures, is in perpetual motion and lateration."

But in spite of continuous motion and secretion in the language, the speaker never loses the feeling of mastering the whole system of his language, because this system never changes too dramatically during his lifetime: what one calls *Sprachgefühl,* feeling for the language, is the instinctive awareness, given to the individual speaker, of an existing equilibrium, of the range of possibilities within the given system which, however, he himself, with every utterance, helps unconsciously to extend or alter. Sometimes he may, by the ironical use of an innovation which he personally rejects, give citizenship papers to an undesirable: witness the hesitant introduction in our contemporary parlance of the word *know-how* whose originally ironical quotation marks tend gradually to disappear. Language as Wilhelm von Humboldt has said is not an ἔργον but an ἐνέργεια, an ever-moving force, not a constituted fact, but there exists also a stable aspect to the language—or else we could have no descriptive grammars— which mirrors indeed man's illusion that his language stands still, just as he thought for so many centuries that his earth stands still; only in the case of language he prefers ironically enough to ignore the fact that he himself is the most assiduous promoter of change. Only when the historical linguist looks back at centuries of development of a language, for instance at the development of English since the time of Chaucer, is he forced to envisage the element of change, which he recognizes by calling the former stage by a different name, such as Middle English. The historian of language may even have a tendency to exaggerate the amount of change in the course of time: there are many features in our living languages which in fact have remained unchanged for millennia: the opposition French *je suis - il est* reflects the Latin opposition *sum - est*, which dates back at least 3,500 years. The historical study of the past stages of a living language gives us, then, insight into that delicate mixture of innovation and conservatism which makes up the texture of a language, as indeed of all human institutions.

One may compare the modern stage of a language not only with its own past, but also with other languages with which some kinship exists. The kinship can be of a threefold kind: *cultural, genealogical,* and *elementarily human.* The cultural kinship in linguistics is what in anthropology would be called ' acculturation ': a superior civilization tends to extend itself to an inferior one and generally, along with the new concept elaborated by that superior civilization, the words in which this concept is formulated tend to be borrowed. Thus while English *horse* is a Germanic word, *chivalry* and *chivalric* are of French origin because the cultural development of *chivalry* was developed in France. These are examples of the so-called " loanwords " which testify to the cultural dependence of the community that borrows upon a superior community that lends. Sometimes it is not the material phonetic form, only the semantics of a loanword that is borrowed: whereas in the case of the *x* of algebra our modern languages have borrowed the whole word, phonetic form and meaning, from the Arabs, the word *square* in its arithmetical use shows only the semantics of its ultimate Greek source *tetragone*. Nearly all the abstract terms current in modern languages are either phonetic or semantic loanwords elaborated by that Greco-Roman-Christian civilization which is the basis of Occidental cultural life. The modern biological and sociological technical term *environment* is a coinage of Carlyle's intended to translate Goethe's term *Umwelt*— which in turn is a translation from Newton's *circumambient medium* and Galileo's *l'ambiente*, themselves expressions ultimately harking back to Greek *to periechon* (" that which encompasses and embraces," meaning alternatively, the air, space, or the world spirit) . Similarly the French term *milieu*, originally *milieu ambiant*, reflects the *circumambient medium* of Newton and through this the Greek term *periechon*. It has been said by naturalists that the dust floating in the air over any one particular area contains particles which have gathered from the whole world; it is equally true that in any particular modern European language there are found loanwords from all over the world: the semantic dust that favorable winds of civilization have brought to us from all over, but especially from ancient Greece.

Genealogical kinship, different from cultural kinship, is based on an uninterrupted continuity of speech as exemplified by the Romance languages which directly continue Latin and are indeed a Neolatin—or by Latin itself, which along with Greek, ProtoGermanic, etc., directly continues the lost, but reconstructable Indo-European language. Whereas in the case of cultural kinship we are able to evaluate the debt, for example, of the English language to other civilizations, in the case of genealogical kinship we sense what English has in common with other descendants from the same Proto-Germanic and Indo-European ancestry. Sometimes an irregularity of English can best be explained by recourse to other members of the Indo-European family which may show a system in full vigor that tends to disappear in our language. Thus English has mainly lost the Indo-European distinction of cases such as nominative and accusative, preserving it only in pronouns (which generally belong to the most conservative part of the language) ; I am alluding to the difference between *who* nominative and *whom* accusative which tends to disappear in modern substandard English, a differentiation having its exact counterpart in Latin *quis - quem,* in harmony with the general opposition nominative-accusative in the declension of nouns: *ignis - ignem.* The confusion between *who* and *whom* which recently marred the text of a law passed by the New York State Legislature could have been avoided had the lawmakers become familiar in their youth with that Latin distinction. A professor of English once told me, when I insisted on the importance of Latin for the development of the grammatical sense in English-speaking students: " How will you teach Latin to students to whom I have not been able all my life to explain the difference between *who* and *whom?* " My answer was of course: " It is because they do not know Latin that they fail to distinguish between *who* and *whom*."

The third kind of linguistic kinship is based on *elementary human nature.* All languages are akin *qua* human languages, that is as reflections of the general human mind. For instance onomatopoeias are found in all languages, although, as we have said, the particular onomatopoeias chosen for a certain concept may vary from language to language. Also, certain negative features, or hesitancies, which we find in a particular language may reflect a general human attitude toward the concept expressed—the attitude toward the future tense being a case in point: many languages lack a particular form for the future and replace it by the present, for instance colloquial German and in part Russian. Indo-European possessed a future tense characterized by an -*s*- infix, as the daughter-languages Greek, Indo-Iranian, and Lithuanian testify, but the -*s*- future of ancient Greek is lost in Neo-Greek which has built a new future from a modal expression ' I will ' reminiscent of English.

In English, the future tense is obviously a relatively recent creation, not firmly cemented as an expression of time relation, as is shown by the alternation in its paradigm of *shall* and *will* (modal expressions which still sometimes retain their original sense: *thou shalt not kill, will you sit down?*) ; in addition the *shall* and *will* future can be freely replaced by *going to* (or, less freely, by the present tense: *the ship sails tomorrow*). In comparison with this loosely knit English future tense, the Latin future (*cantabo-faciam*), with its exclusive reference to future time, may seem to show an imposing precision; but to the closer inspection of the comparatist it is revealed as originating in modal expressions parallel to the English formation: *faciam facies* are originally subjunctives and optative formations meaning ' I may do, may you do,' and *cantabo* is originally a compound meaning ' I become singing ' (comparable to standard German *ich werde singen*), in which *bo* is a separate verb related to Greek φύομαι, English *to be*. In other words, Latin which had lost the Indo-European *s*- future built it up again by means of modal expressions in the same manner as English and Neo-Greek have done. Again the Latin paradigms, seemingly so well-established, did not survive in Romance which rebuilt new futures by means of modal verbs: French *je chanterai* is a *cantare habeo* ' I have to sing '; in Romanian the future is expressed by ' I wish to sing '; in Sardinian by ' I must sing.' Finally, in French, the future tense is today on the point of disintegration, being replaced either by the present or by ' going to ' (*je vais chanter*), in dialects by ' I will.'

Why do we witness in the history of Latin and Neolatin

(e. g. French) a thrice-repeated pendulum movement of alternatively building up a future tense and then destroying it (the Indo-European *s-* future yielding to *cantabo*, this in turn yielding to *cantare habeo* > *je chanterai*, this in turn to *je vais chanter*) ? A comparison with non-Indo-European phenomena shows that we are faced with a generally human fact: the ambiguous attitude of man toward the future: he approaches it over and over again with his emotions (his will, his feelings of duty, his self-reliance or fear of destiny), allowing the modal expressions to crystallize into neat intellectual expressions of the time relationship, only to let these again disintegrate and to replace them by new popular expressions tinged with emotion—and the pendulum movement may start over again. The English future tense is then only one among many manifestations of the ontological hesitancy of man, when faced with the future, between an intellectual and an emotional attitude. In its behavior toward the future tense the English language is less English than *language*, human language. It is such insights into both the continuity and variety of man's nature that give the historical linguist that *divin piacere*, that delight worthy of the gods, which Vico felt to be the prerogative of the historian or, in Jakob Burckhardt's image: historical consciousness makes us equal to the man on top of the mountain who senses, in what seems dissonance for the inhabitants of the valley, the greatest harmony.

Montesquieu's Parisian bourgeoisie (who surely lived in the valley), when faced with an influx of Persians into their capital, naively asked: "How can one be a Persian?" Comparative linguistics teaches indeed that one *can* be a Persian; this science is anti-bourgeois, anti-Babbitt in its essence; it reflects a civilized art of remembering the manifoldness and the range of human behavior.

The young student who is laboriously trying to decipher a Greek or Latin sentence with its network of dependent clauses, participles and indirect discourse extending perhaps over a whole page, might draw some comfort from the thought that an ancient Greek or Roman would have had equal trouble with an English sentence with its cluster of prepositions such as: " Mama, what did you bring that book that I didn't want to be read to out of up for? " The mental gymnastics imposed on any deciphering of a foreign language text, ancient or modern, is a healthy training in the understanding of any *human context*, in that *understanding* characteristic of the humanities. This effort is of a particular kind, quite different from the procedure in mathematics in which one deduces consequences from a few, very simple axioms which have been isolated from the whole of reality. In any deciphering one is faced with a whole network of difficulties which present themselves in a lump at the same time: words, word-meanings, constructions, in themselves perhaps known to us, must be fitted together into that unique mosaic which alone makes sense—and, in addition (and this is again quite different from mathematics, which, once it has left the realm of outward reality, need not return to it) , the particular outward situation described in the text may be unknown to us: the meaning of the text may become clear not by the *Sprachgefühl* for the particular language alone, but only by the additional application of our general human experience which may tell us which word-meanings and which constructions might fit the outward situation described in the text.

In order to penetrate this linguistic-situational web, we can only form for ourselves a tentative, rapidly anticipated hypothesis about the meaning of the whole passage, based on some details which we have immediately apperceived; then we may verify our quick assumption by taking up more slowly all the details, linguistic as well as situational, to see whether all of them fit our first hypothesis: only when they do have we guessed right. This is a circular operation, not at all a vicious circle, but the basic operation in all the humanities, in history or literature as well as in philology: it consists in starting from certain details and attempting to establish a synthetic view of the whole, later to verify whether all the details can be explained from the assumed meaning of the whole. Significantly enough, the so-called "circle of understanding in the humanities" was discovered by the German classical philologist and Platonistic philosopher Schleiermacher when he attempted to explain to himself the criteria by which to proceed in the deciphering of obscure passages in Homer, and it is the method by which all deciphering and even the modern decoding techniques are guided—and if the work of American counter-intelligence in the last war that was able to save thousands of lives, has demonstrated to the whole nation a possibility of practical application of the humanities, an applicability which was equal to that of the sciences (if not equally advertised), it must be remembered that our counter-intelligence experts were using the methods of Homeric textual criticism.

But language study offers not only lessons of tolerance and a training in humanistic understanding. It also teaches us to appraise the power of language on thought, the power of the collective subconscious, as latent in the language, even in our enlightened modern civilization. Every language offers to its speakers a ready-made *interpretation* of the world, truly a *Weltanschauung*, a *metaphysical* word-picture which, after having originated in the thinking of our ancestors, tends to impose itself ever anew on posterity. Take for instance a simple sentence such as ' I see him,' in which the personal and transitive use of the verb is the same as in ' I kill him,' ' I throw it away.' This means that English and, I might say, Indo-European, presents the impressions made on our senses predominantly as human *activities,* brought about by our *will.* But the Eskimos in Greenland say not 'I see him' but 'he appears to me,' just as they say in the other cases just mentioned: 'he dies to me,' 'it flies away from me.' Thus the Indo-European speaker conceives as workings of his activities what the fatalistic Eskimo sees as events that happen to him. But in our Indo-European languages traces of the 'happening' type of expressions for inner experiences are not missing: in Latin one said for 'I dreamed,' 'it was seen by me in a dream'; a Russian must say in this case 'it dreamed itself to me'; and, in English, 'I remember,' which has taken the place of a former 'it remembers me,' may still today alternate with the impersonal 'it occurs to me'; German, the "language of dreamers" has a series of impersonal expressions such as *es träumt, ahnt, schwant, deucht mir* along with *ich träume ahne, denke*—all of which means that our Indo-European languages, some more, some less, still reflect an earlier cultural period where man conceived himself as more subject to action from outside then as capable of action of his own, more sensorial than motoric. Indeed, 'it occurs to me' is of the same impersonal type as that found in the meteorological expressions 'it is raining, snowing' in which obviously man refrains from asserting any action on his part. When Lichtenberg opposed Descartes' statement 'I think, therefore I am' by pointing out that the French philosopher had too lightly assumed the existence of a thinking ego on the basis of a speech habit which presents thinking as action on the part of the thinker, while he should have said 'it thinks in me,' he was reminding us, perhaps influenced by his native German, of that ancient irrational subsoil of the human ego which still lingers in us below the Cartesian pride of reason.

Now how should we explain the meteorological impersonal verbs with which we compared the type 'it occurs to me'? Comparative linguistics teaches us that Greek impersonals such as ὕει ('it is raining') and βροντᾷ ('it is thundering') were originally simple *nouns* meaning 'rain!' 'thunder!'—that is, emotional exclamations stating nothing but the existence of the meteorological phenomenon. But as old as these remainders of purely phenomenalistic expression are expressions such as Ζεὺς ὕει, βροντᾷ ('Zeus is raining, thundering'), Zeus being an Indo-European God, *Dyaus-pitā* in Sanskrit, *Juppiter* in Latin, the Father-God of the bright shining day, who when he pleases can become the *Juppiter Tonans*. By these expressions an agent, a supernatural agent is posited to whom the outward events can be retraced. With the sentence 'Zeus is raining' man has attempted a first step toward science, to find causation in the cosmos, an explanation of the world by a myth: he has reached the first stage of science which the positivistic philosopher Auguste Comte has called the theological stage. Many languages still today show the imprint of that religious stage—for example in Hungarian one says for 'it is raining': 'the rainer is raining.'

The second stage of science according to Comte is the 'metaphysical' one, in which occult natural forces or impersonal essences are assumed as causes: this stage is linguistically reflected by the 'it' in our modern type of expression 'it is raining,' where 'it' is a force x outside of us, considered as an agent. The third stage of science is reached, according to Comte, in the modern era of positivism when man no longer explains the world by anthropomorphic theology or vague metaphysics, but by the sense-data accessible to him and by their controllable relationships: but one will notice that this stage has not yet penetrated into our common speech which remains bound by theological or metaphysical tradition, 'uncorrected' by science in the sense of Lichtenberg and Condillac: we still do not say for 'it is raining': 'condensed atmospheric vapor is falling in drops,' just as we still continue, in spite of Copernicus, to say *the sun rises,* or *sets.* In Neo-Greek the phrase 'the sun is setting' is rendered by 'the sun is enthroned like a king,' in Romanian by 'the sun enters into sainthood'; in both cases the splendor and glory of the natural phenomenon is interpreted in terms of the human-superhuman splendor characteristic of Byzantine art. Similarly, although it would seem possible only in primitive prelogical animistic thinking that sex could be attributed to inanimate things, the majority of European languages have up to today retained grammatical gender ('water' is feminine in French *eau* as it was in Latin *aqua*). Language is then not satisfied with denoting factual contents, but forces the speakers to adopt certain metaphysical or religious interpretations of the world which the community may have learnt to deny. These obsolete conceptions remain latent in the language: just as Aeneas when all hope was lost carried his father out of burning Troy on his shoulders, so we tend to espouse our forefathers' beliefs and words in any emergency—when we will react atavistically: even atheists will then ejaculate *God!* and Voltaire has a libertine Swiss colonel pray in the stress of battle: "God, if you exist, save my soul, if I have one!"

The atavistic prelogical residue in our language, which may constitute a danger for the scientist unaware of the semantic fallacies of the latter (unaware, that is, of the "history of ideas" underlying our language), can however be used deliberately and with great aesthetic effect in literary art—in poetry.

When we hear in the refrain of a folksong inserted by Shakespeare into one of his plays the line "The rain it raineth every-day," we have the vague feeling that, although the factual content is no different from that of the conventional phrase 'it rains everyday,' the form chosen presents the fact in a slightly new light. There is here posited an irrational power that raineth: 'the rain rains' is indeed a quite unusual expression in modern English (though not in Hungarian, as we have said), suggestive, as it were, of another world than the one we are familiar with. In addition, certain linguistic and prosodic devices tend to enforce the impression that we have entered a world at the same time our own and not our own: the archaic ending *-eth* in *raineth*, which evokes times immemorial; the iambic rythm here suggesting the monotony of perpetually falling rain (*the rain it ráineth évery dáy*); the repetition of the stem *rain* which reinforces the impression of monotony. Here then the arbitrary character of our words has been annulled and a particular significance has been given to the acoustic impression which has indeed become expressive of meaning. Thus words which had meaning only by convention (θέσει) have been made to express meaning in correspondence with their sound (φύσει).

I have quoted a line of Shakespeare, which is surely not one of the most inspired, in order to show some basic elements required in the transformation of language by poetry: we found in that line a repristination of a mythological concept, symbolized by linguistic devices destined to give motivation to the arbitrary words of the language—and that is precisely what poetry generally achieves: to produce, by language-constructs differing from normal speech, adumbrations of a metaphysical world in which the laws of science, causality, practicality, as we know them and need them in our workaday world, seem no longer to obtain and in which we vaguely come to visualize *other* laws.

Indeed, the account of the creation in Genesis (which conflicts with evolutionistic modern science) is couched in a poetic language whose spell still today acts on all of us with undiminished force: "And God said: *Let there be light, and there was light "*—the power of this line which already the pagan rhetorician Longinus had recognized as an example of what he called " the sublime," that is, the grandiose expressed simply, resides in the word-parallelisms of the two sentences, and in the use of the conjunction ' and,' as a result of which the command of God is presented as leading inevitably and naturally to its own fulfilment. In the Hebrew original the parallelism is even more complete because the same verb-form serves for both the command and the fulfilment: *jĕhī aur va-jĕhī aur.* That miracle of miracles, the creation of light, has become simple, self-evident *poetic* reality. Here the onomatopoeia restored by poetry is much subtler and much more discreet than in the reproduction of the melody of rain in Shakespeare's refrain.

It is even possible for poetry to evoke the rhythm of purely abstract thought. While it is relatively easy to compose poetry about love and spring, subject matters in themselves naturally poetic, the greatest challenge is offered to the poet when he proposes, as Lucretius and Dante have done, to sing of subject matter most rebellious to poetry, of abstract philosophical thought: " to make ideas sing " (in Valéry's words). I shall choose a relatively small poetic organism in order to show how, by means of delicate prosodic devices, a philosophical idea can be made poetry: the sonnet of the Idea by the French poet Du Bellay (published in 1549). According to Plato the human soul is provided with wings wherewith to fly toward heaven, where dwells the divine idea of beauty, wisdom and goodness: the true reality of which all earthly beauty, wisdom and goodness is only an imperfect copy. Let us see now how the Renaissance poet has converted this Platonic myth, which is itself a poetic description of man's constant aspiration toward the ideal, into *pure poetry:*

> *Si nostre vie est moins qu'une journée*
> *En l'éternel, si l'an qui faict le tour*
> *Chasse noz jours sans espoir de retour,*
> *Si perissable est toute chose née,*
>
> *Que songes-tu, mon ame emprisonnée?*
> *Pourquoy te plaist l'obscur de nostre jour,*
> *Si pour voler en un plus cler sejour,*
> *Tu as au dos l'aele bien empanée?*
>
> *La est le bien que tout esprit desire,*
> *La le repos ou tout le monde aspire,*
> *La est l'amour, la le plaisir encore,*
>
> *La, ô mon ame au plus hault ciel guidée,*
> *Tu y pouras recognoistre l'Idée*
> *De la beauté qu'en ce monde j'adore.*

The aesthetic secret of the sonnet seems to lie in the fact that the soul's striving toward the Idea is not only *stated* as in Plato's prose, but *enacted* with the help of certain linguistic devices. Du Bellay has here achieved an extraordinary convergence between rythm and sentence structure on the one hand, and the content developed in the poem on the other, with the result that the reader feels unconsciously drawn by the language of the poem into a movement of the latter's—which, as we come to the end, is revealed to reflect the attractive force of the Platonic idea. Not only do the words suggest the upward movement, but rhythm and syntax encourage the reader who recites the poem to imitate this movement by modulation of his own voice, by musical intonation. Modulation and pitch are normally given with all speech, but the art of the poet consists in inducing us to use these devices in harmony with the content—*expressively*. It would be impossible for any reader to read the poem, or for any composer to put it into music, except by starting in a low register and raising steadily the pitch until finally, in the last two lines, the Idea of Beauty is revealed to us in the Empyreum—the rise of pitch becoming symbolic of the flight of the soul toward ever higher spheres. Similarly, the sentence structure in the first quatrain with its restlessly striving three incidental clauses reflects the restlessness man may feel in his earthly prison, even before the word *emprisonnée* in the main clause (l. 9) will spell out the nature of our existence.

In the second stanza, with the two questions of benevolent admonishment, there is already given a suggestion of liberation: to the motif of the prison are now opposed the motifs of 'wing and flight'—and liberation is *realized* with the first *là* ('there') of stanza 3, which everyone will read with great energy (Là *est le bien que tout esprit désire*) as if the soul had already broken its chains in an upward movement toward salvation, and the sight of the goal were identical with the flight toward it. All the restlessness of the two first stanzas is now transcended: in the traditionally shorter second half of the sonnet there is represented the fulfilment of the desires described in the first half. The elation that goes with liberation now manifests itself in an *accelerando*, in a new restlessness, parallel to the earlier one, yet totally different in nature: the five times repeated demonstrative adverbs *là* . . . *là* . . . ('there . . . there') are like rungs on a foreshortened ladder that leads straight toward the goal. The movement in these stanzas quickens and becomes *staccato*, in breathless anticipation of that infinite and unlimited enjoyment felt by the soul at the moment of the Epiphany of the Idea; and with this supernatural appearance calm and serenity at last prevail, as they are depicted in a double line that is indeed *one* sweeping long line corresponding to the triumph, elation, transfiguration of the soul that has reached its goal:

> *Tu y pourras reconnaître l'Idée*
> *de la Beauté qu'en ce monde j'adore.*

L'idée de la Beauté is the apex of the poem, the zenith, as the nadir was *notre vie* in line 1, and also the highest point reached by the reader's voice—which, immediately after, will fall, as the soul, glancing backward on the stretch of way it has traversed, is able to discern now on this earth, *ce monde*, reflections or copies of the archetype of the Idea of Beauty. The final note in this cyclical poem in which indeed " the poet's eye, in a fine frenzy rolling doth glance from heaven to earth and from earth to heaven," is no longer one of contempt of this earth, but rather of reconciliation with our world which now appears transfigured by the poet's experience of heavenly beauty. The verb *j'adore*, to be sounded in a low register with calm emotion, that must somehow linger beyond the end of the poem, suggests a religious attitude, sustained, confidently established beyond all danger of the abyss.

Now all the lexicological, rhythmical, syntactical, and structural devices by which Du Bellay has succeeded in embodying an abstract philosophical idea, the attraction of man by the world of ideas, are at bottom due to that basic phenomenon inherent in human language, *expressivity*, but which here has been extended and intensified by the poet so as to produce in us the illusion of an ' as if '—a world in which the myths of yore come true. The desire for illusion, for surcease from the laws of causality is indeed deep-rooted in all of us: On the lowest level, in an age of mass civilization and of timidity of imagination, this desire will send many to the comic strips which give them the distinterested enjoyment of a world which, while freed from the modern implications of determinism and transfigured by the comic spirit or the spirit of adventure, can still somehow be felt to be *their own world* (and many will turn to the world of the Shmoos, those word-born beings that have developed out of the Yiddish word for ' profit, illicit gain ' into prototypes of that abundance and goodness of the earth which is freely given to all men) ; on the highest level, the more boldly imaginative reader will enjoy Dante's crushing or elevating picture of an *entirely imaginary* world with a physics and a biology quite aberrant from our own, wherein it is love that moves the sun and the stars, and where the disembodied souls live in the presence of God, while miraculously retaining their earthly physical appearance and emotion.

But, we might ask, must man, in order to free himself by poetry from the prison of his actual environment, always take refuge in the poetry of past ages which necessarily embodies obsolete mythological and cosmological conceptions? Could modern man never turn to poetry that would express modern scientific truth with all its metaphysical implications, endowed with that artistic beauty and that realistic evidence which in Dante compels belief? Is the life-giving power of poetry reserved only for sublime folly, which makes real what the poet believes he knows, is it denied to the sober wisdom of truth that truly knows? The fact that there has not yet appeared a modern Dante who would make modern science sing (who would, that is, make science appear as belonging both to our own and to a transmundane world) is, however, easily enough explained: the burden of age-old myths still weighs too heavy on our words to allow them to express the mythology of our time. The greatest modern historian, Arnold Toynbee, the greatest because the most poetic, because he has sensed most keenly the necessity for modern historiography to free us from the doom of history, often has recourse to poetic myth—but his poetic myths are, as Friedrich Engel-Janosi has shown, those of the past (as when Toynbee explains the birth of new civilizations as the answers of a human community to the challenge of the Devil who has invaded the world of God) . It is my personal feeling that the concepts of the moral world, of God and Devil, will not be abandoned altogether in the centuries to come, but will gradually be rephrased and shaded in consonance with our scientific knowledge of the physical world. After all, Dante's poetic codification of medieval science and its synthesis with Christian theology came 1,500 years after the poetic codification by Lucretius of pagan untheological science. We should then restrain our modern impatience and wait for another 1,500 years for the poetic language to mature that would furnish adequate instruments for the expression of the scientific world-picture of Einstein and Curie and of the religious implications this may have. The mills of language grind slow, but they grind exceedingly fine.

I hope I have been able to show that language is not only a banal means of communication and self-expression, but also one of orientation in this world: a way that leads toward science and is perfected by science, and on the other hand also a means for freeing us from this world thanks to its metaphysical and poetic implications. Language, the raw material of poetry, is distinguished from the raw materials of the other arts in that it is already in itself a refined human artistic activity, an *energeia* which embodies meaning in sound produced by the most immaterial and elusive instruments of the human body (our breath playing on delicate keyboards behind the screen of our face). And this same material-immaterial activity: *language*, the main vehicle for communication of meaning in the business of this world, is able to transform itself into the rainbow bridge which leads mankind toward other worlds where meaning rules absolute.

GILBERT CHINARD

Progress and Perfectibility in Samuel Miller's Intellectual History

〉〉〉〉〉〉〉〉〉〉〉〉〉〉〉〉〉〉〉〉〉

As I remember it, the formation of the History of Ideas Club at The Johns Hopkins University was not preceded by any declaration of principles, nor by the adoption of a formal constitution and bylaws. It was essentially a friendly gathering of men who believed in the fundamental unity of knowledge and felt the need of crossing the barriers of administrative and departmental divisions. In fact, it may be said that the Club existed before having a name; it took shape thanks to the catalytic influence of Lovejoy. We had the greatest respect for some of our older colleagues who engaged in what might be called "atomized" research and listened to them patiently and often profitably; but we knew the dangers of overspecialization and we thought that the time had come for experimenting with what Lovejoy called "cross fertilization."

The meetings of the Club were not intended for the presentation of finished papers. Members felt free to submit hypotheses, to venture outside of their designated field, in the hope of getting the suggestions and criticisms of their colleagues. One of the first results of these meetings, for some of us at least, was the demonstration of the polyvalence of terms generally used, the inadequacy of labels, the necessity of sharper distinctions and definitions.

94

The Club might well have taken for its motto, the saying of Montesquieu at the beginning of Book XI of the *Esprit des lois*: " There is no word that has admitted of more various significations, and has made more different impressions on human minds, than that of Liberty." Without a keen analysis of these key words the History of Ideas might easily have degenerated into vague and so-called philosophical disquisitions and generalizations, such as those which gave a bad name to comparative literature or philosophy of history. Fortunately we had a friendly guide and pilot in these intellectual adventures. We soon realized that such terms as Nature, Romanticism, Primitivism, Exoticism, or Evolution, to mention only a few striking illustrations, had many facets and were not to be lightly and loosely used. Through his work more than through precepts and discussions on methodology, Lovejoy stood among us as an extraordinary exemplar.

The author of this essay has often regretted that his connection with the Club has become distant and irregular. The paper presented here, if circumstances had allowed, would and should have been submitted to the Club. It is tentative and exploratory; its only excuse for being written at all is that it may call attention to the need of defining more exactly the many acceptations of a word which became a sort of battle cry during the eighteenth century and expressed in a somewhat nebulous way the ideal of the nineteenth.

On January 1, 1801, at the request of some friends, a young minister of the Presbyterian Church, the Reverend Samuel Miller, delivered a sermon containing an attempt, " on entering a new century to review the preceding, and to deduce from the prominent features of that period such moral and religious reflexions as might be suited to the occasion." Being requested to publish it, he soon formed the very ambitious plan of writing a complete conspectus of the eighteenth century, including theology, morals, politics, natural philosophy, and literature, and "discussing the main events in the Christian church, in the moral world and in political principles and establishments during that century." Three full years were spent in the preparation of the work which was published in January, 1804 (although dated 1803) under the title of:

> *A Brief Retrospect of the Eighteenth Century. Part First; in Two Volumes: containing a Sketch of the Revolutions and Improvements in Science, Arts, and Literature, during that Period.* By Samuel Miller, A. M. One of the Ministers of the United Presbyterian Churches in the City of New York, Member of the American Philosophical Society, and Corresponding Member of the Historical Society of Massachusetts.

This descriptive title fails to give even an approximate idea of the wealth of the documentation contained in these two fat volumes of 560 and 517 pages respectively, with copious footnotes and additions. The table of contents lists twenty-six chapters, ranging from Mechanical Philosophy to a capital discussion of "Nations lately become Literary: Russia, Germany, United States of America."

If we remember that Dr. Miller had intended to discuss in additional volumes, which were never written, the "exciting subject of Politics, as well as the Subjects of Theology and Morals," it will be seen that this summary is far more extensive than the "encyclopedic tree" of Diderot and d'Alembert or Jefferson's tabulation for establishing a library. Truly encyclopedic in its compass, the *Brief Retrospect* is not a dictionary or a dry repertory. In some respects it is compilation, and modestly the author admitted that in many instances he had to be content with second-hand information: "It will not be supposed that the author has attentively read all the works concerning which he delivers opinions. Some of them he never saw, and has ventured to give their character entirely on the authority of those whom he considers better judges than himself. Many he has seen and consulted, with more or less attention, as his avocations allowed."

There is no mystery about the sources of his information: he made use of all the treatises, dictionaries, and encyclopedias he could lay his hands upon; he consulted the best critics and authorities; he borrowed books from the Circulating Library of Caritat and undoubtedly he was assisted by his associates in the Friendly Club. Some of the chapters are highly technical, and we are not aware that the young churchman had pushed very far his investigations in this field. We know for certain that the chapter on medicine was contributed by his brother, Dr. Edward Miller, who may also have advised him on other chapters dealing with natural philosophy. But Samuel Miller was possessed with such an insatiable curiosity that, on his own admission, he managed to obtain at least some " acquaintance " with most of the works he discussed.

In every page, and practically in every paragraph, he injected comments and reflections of his own; his personality was too vivacious and his mind too irrepressible to permit him simply to report accepted opinions. A staunch Presbyterian of unwavering faith and unimpeachable conduct, he never hesitated to give the Devil his due. While gathering material for the *Retrospect*, he actively engaged in the fierce battle between Federalists and Republicans, declaring himself unequivocally for Jefferson in terms which he later bitterly regretted:

> I profess to be a Christian. I wish all men were Christians. We should have more private, social and political happiness. But what then? Because Mr. Jefferson is suspected of Deism, are we to raise a hue and cry against him, as if he ought to be instantly deprivated of his rights of

citizenship? If he be an infidel, I lament it for two reasons: from a concern for his own personal salvation, and that a religion, which is so much spoken against, does not receive his countenance and aid. But notwithstanding this, I think myself perfectly consistent in saying that I had much rather have Mr. Jefferson President of the United States, than an aristocratic Christian (*Life*, I, 131).

His attitude towards authors and scientists suspected of infidelity or known to be infidels is defined in a similar vein in the Preface to the *Brief Retrospect*:

Should any reader be offended by the language of panegyric which is frequently bestowed on the intellectual and scientific endowments of some distinguished abettors of heresy or of infidelity, he is entreated to remember that justice is due to all men. A man who is a bad Christian may be a very excellent mathematician, astronomer, or chemist; and one who denies and blasphemes the Saviour may write profoundly and instructively on some branches of science highly interesting to mankind. It is proper to commiserate the mistakes of such persons, to abhor their blasphemy, and to warn men against their fatal delusions; but it is surely difficult to see either justice or utility of withholding from them that praise of genius or of learning to which they are fairly entitled (I, xii-xiii).

And so it happened that, when discussing the improvements of the English language during the eighteenth century, Samuel Miller referred unexpectedly to a rank infidel:

There are some good remarks on English style in the *Inquirer, a Series of Essays*, by WILLIAM GODWIN. Though no friend to human happiness can recommend the moral or religious principles of this writer, which are pre-eminently fitted to delude, corrupt and destroy; yet he is himself master of a vigourous style, and his judgment on a question of literary taste is entitled to respect (II, 101).

No less remarkable is his appreciation of Buffon's theory of the earth, which had aroused the ire of the Paris theologians:

> Such are the outlines of a theory bold and plausible, as might have been expected from the mind of its author, but unsubstantial and deceptive. Its manifest object is to exclude the agency of a Divine Architect, and to represent a world begun and perfected merely by the operation of natural, undesigning causes. That it cannot be reconciled with the sacred history, will appear evident on the slightest inspections; and that it involves the grossest absurdities has been clearly shown by successive geologists. It was embraced, however, by M. BAILLY, of France, by the celebrated HOLLMAN, of Goettingen, and others; and continues to be respected and adopted by many to the present time (I, 167).

At a time when the names of Voltaire and Rousseau had become anathema in political and religious circles, Samuel Miller was one of the very few churchmen who had enough courage and objectivity to refuse to pronounce a wholesale condemnation of their works. As a budding historian, he had looked for models among his predecessors and he was aware of the real revolution undergone by historiography during the last half of the eighteenth century: " the best historians have interwoven with their narratives of political and military events, much amusing and valuable information, concerning the religion, learning, laws, customs, trade and every other object tending to throw light on the progress, genius and conditions of different communities." Speeches and other extraneous matter have been excluded by the best historians from the body of their works and the modern reader can now appreciate " how intimately revolutions, and other national events are often connected with the current of literary, moral, and religious opinions; and how much a knowledge of one is frequently fitted to elucidate the other." This remarkable improvement was largely due to a man who was "endowed with an uncommon share of wit, humour, fancy, and taste," and who had "enjoyed a high reputation, not only as an epic poet, but also as a dramatist, an historian, a novelist, an essayist, and a miscellaneous writer." It was to be lamented that his talents "were so much devoted to the cause of impiety and licentiousness," but it had to be recognized that "the author to whom we are probably more indebted than to any other individual, for introducing and recommending this improvement in civil history, is M. VOLTAIRE. His *Age of Louis XIV*, was one of the first specimens of a work upon this plan."

These few quotations, which could be multiplied, may serve to illustrate Samuel Miller's historical and critical method. Obviously he thought that as an historian he had to record a consensus of opinion on a given author, while preserving his right to express, often in his footnotes, a severe denunciation on moral grounds of productions otherwise highly regarded. The *Brief Retrospect* was written and published at a time when the battle between the partisans of the French "*philosophes*" and the defenders of orthodoxy was still raging and when very few writers or, for that matter, churchmen preserved a calm judgment. In fact, in this respect, the *Brief Retrospect* stands by itself.

It offers another even more uncommon merit. While European writers like Madame de Staël were striving to divest themselves of national prejudices and to judge of European culture as a whole, not even the woman often regarded as the founder of comparative literature was able to forget or do away with traditional attitudes and prejudices. To say that Samuel Miller was a better "European" than the author of the book just published under the title of *De la littérature considérée dans ses rapports avec les mœurs et les institutions sociales*, may seem paradoxical and yet the paradox is only apparent. For reasons which need no elaboration, Miller knew more about England than about any other country. He admitted that his knowledge of continental Europe was very rudimentary. He probably read French easily; it is very doubtful that he had any German; and his acquaintance with Italian and Spanish was exceedingly slight. But it is remarkable that, when he brought together the results of his inquiry on what may be called the intellectual state of Europe, he refused to recognize any territorial division. The chapters of the *Brief Retrospect* cut across all frontiers and are treated as subdivisions of the great republic of letters which transcends all national distinctions. Thus it happened that the very remoteness of his situation and his keen interest in all matters of knowledge combined to make of Miller not only a " good European," but a true cosmopolitan in the broadest sense of the word.

In addition he was a very good American. While the achievements of distinguished Americans are listed in the *Brief Retrospect* as part of the contribution of his fellow-countrymen to the general development of knowledge, Miller took care to sum up these achievements by themselves at the end of several chapters. In his concluding chapters he abondoned his general or international method of exposition to treat separately of three nations which during the eighteenth century had risen " from obscurity in the republic of letters, to a considerable literary and scientific eminence ";—namely Russia, Germany, and the United States of America. In studying such a striking phenomenon, Miller was eager not only to do justice to his country but to test and verify his theory of history and to " correlate " historical and social events with the progress of intellectual activities and the diffusion of knowledge.

Without attempting to give a résumé of these ninety pages full of facts, which constitute a complete intellectual history of the United States from the origins to the end of the eighteenth century, I shall simply recall that it was part and parcel of the campaign started around 1780 by Benjamin Franklin in France and Thomas Jefferson, still in his native Virginia, to define the character of the society and culture which had arisen in the New World. Miller presented no extravagant claims. He was especially anxious to call his fellow-countrymens' attention to what remained to be done and to the measures to be taken to bring American culture to a fuller development. He conceded that " what is called a *liberal education* in the United States " was, " in common, less accurate and complete " than in Great Britain and in " some of the more enlightened nations on the Eastern continent." This situation was not to be attributed to any deficiency of native talent, nor, contrary to Buffon's theory, to " any inaptitude in its soil or atmosphere to promote the growth of genius," but to well-defined causes which in part could be remedied: " Defective plans and means of instruction in our Seminaries of learning; Want of leisure; Want of encouragement to learning; Want of Books." Another unfavorable condition was the constant comparison established between the productions of England and the literary efforts of the United States, which tended to discourage many authors. Moreover, " Americans are too apt to join with ignorant or fastidious foreigners, in undervaluing and decrying our domestic literature; and this circumstance is one of the numerous obstacles which have operated to discourage literary exertions on this side of the Atlantic, and to impede our literary progress."

The conclusion, however, is optimistic, for Miller firmly believed that these baneful influences would gradually diminish. His prophecy is worth recording:

> The number of learned men is becoming rapidly greater.
> . . . A larger proportion of the growing wealth of our
> country will hereafter be devoted to the improvement of

knowledge, and especially to the furtherance of all means
by which scientific discoveries are brought within popular
reach, and rendered subservient to practical utility. . . .
[The time is coming near] when we shall be able to make
some return to our transatlantic brethren, for the rich
stores of useful knowledge, which they have been pouring
upon us for nearly two centuries (II, 409-410).

This bright prospect for America brings to a close Miller's
general survey of the eighteenth century. It is truly an astonishing achievement and yet it seems to have been completely ignored
by recent literary historians. As far as I have been able to ascertain, Merle Curti, in his book on *The Growth of American
Thought* (1943 and 1951) was the first to pay a long overdue
tribute to his forgotten predecessor.

The first monumental work devoted solely to this field
[intellectual history] appeared in 1803, when the Reverend
Samuel Miller, a Presbyterian clergyman of New York, published his two-volume *Retrospect of the Eighteenth Century.*
This series of essays on virtually every phase of the intellectual life of Europe in the eighteenth century included
surveys of the state of knowledge in the United States and
of American contributions to knowledge. With all its
shortcomings it was a notable effort and is still useful to
the student of the growth of American thought (p. ix).

More recently this high praise of Samuel Miller was echoed by
John Higham, in an article on " The Rise of American Intellectual History" (*American Historical Review*, April 1951).
Going much farther than Merle Curti, Mr. Higham does not
hesitate to see in Samuel Miller an American representative of
the enlightenment, a statement which, as we shall see, cannot be
accepted without strong reservations.

History of thought assumes a central importance in historical study as Voltaire, Condorcet, and others celebrated the

progress of humanity and the power of reason as its driving force. To these apostles of Enlightenment, the record of human intelligence in the past had an altogether new significance, it confirmed their faith in a progressive future.

The first American to study systematically the materials of intellectual history performed a similar function and bore a similar debt to the impulse of the Enlightenment. In surveying advances in twenty arts and sciences, Samuel Miller's *Brief Retrospect of the Eighteenth Century* (1803) showed caution as well as learning; but it testified in every chapter to the triumphs of progress and reason . . . (p. 454).

A closer analysis of Samuel Miller's views of the doctrine of progress will show that these resemblances are superficial and call for essential qualifications.

Very significantly Miller carefully avoided the use of the term "progress" in the title of his book, substituting for it the word "revolution," by which he meant considerable changes and even unprecedented changes. But in his introduction he refused to commit himself, pointing out significantly that it was extremely difficult to distinguish "between revolution and improvement." "Who can undertake to say in what cases these are synonymous terms, and when they are directly opposite? If every change were to be considered an advantage, it would follow, of course, that the strides of civilized man, in every species of improvement, during the last century, have been prodigious. But alas! this principle cannot be admitted by the cautious inquirer, or the friend of human happiness."

In the century which had just come to a close he saw "much to deplore and much to admire," an unusual number of revolutions, and "at least some improvements." This might serve as a conclusion to practically every chapter in the first volume which deals with the "revolutions" the eighteenth century had witnessed in the realm of science, and the material features of human life. We may take as an illustration the chapter on chemistry. According to Miller, from a source of amusement and an object of curiosity, chemistry had been converted into a most instructive, interesting and valuable science. " There is scarcely an art of human life which it is not fitted to subserve; scarcely a department of human inquiry or labour, either for health, pleasure, ornament, or profit which it may not be made, in its present improved state eminently to promote." (I, 108)

This is simply the recognition of a fact and common knowledge. But such a recognition does not imply the approval of " chemical philosophy" and of the extravagant votaries of chemistry who " have undertaken, on chemical principles, to account for all the phenomena of *motion, life* and *mind,* and on those very facts which clearly prove wise design, and the super-intending care of an INFINITE INTELLIGENCE, have attempted to build a fabric of *atheistical* philosophy. This is a remarkable instance of those *oppositions of science falsely so called,* of which an inspired writer speaks, and for which the past age has been remarkably distinguished." (I, 110)

Having clearly defined and limited the realm of science, which to him, as to Benjamin Franklin and his colleagues of the American Philosophical Society, consisted essentially in " useful knowledge," Samuel Miller experienced no difficulty in granting that everyday life has undergone an unprecedented transformation during the eighteenth century. These changes had come with dramatic suddenness, particularly in America, and in his praise of that scientific revolution Samuel Miller was second to none:

> When we compare the ancient modes of living, with the dress, the furniture, the equipage, the conveniences of travelling, and the incomparable greater ease with which the same amount of comfortable accommodation may be obtained at present, none can hesitate to give a decided preference in all these respects, to modern times. Perhaps it

would not be extravagant to say that many of the higher orders of mechanics and day labourers now wear better clothes, and live, not more plentifully, but in some respects more conveniently, more neatly, and with more true taste, than many princes and kings were in the habit of doing two centuries ago, and in a manner quite as pleasant as multitudes of a rank far superior to themselves, at a later period. In short, the remarkable and unprecedented union of neatness and simplicity, cheapness, and elegance, which has been exhibited, in the art of living, within thirty or forty years, is, at once, a testimony of the rapid improvement of the mechanic arts, and one of the most unquestionable points in which we may claim a superiority over our predecessors. (I, 403)

Thus spake the American and the friend of Jefferson, for no European at that date would have been justified in drawing such a glowing picture of the new way of life brought about by the conquests of science. Whether the great improvements in the physical sciences had been accompanied with corresponding improvements in " the science of the human mind and the auxiliary branches of philosophy " was really the crux of the problem. Samuel Miller intended to discuss it under its different aspects and to treat particularly of the political, social and religious consequences and significance of the " revolutions " which had taken place during the eighteenth century. He never completed his survey of this enormous field; but the second volume of the *Brief Retrospect* makes sufficiently clear the main lines of his doctrine.

He started with a chapter on the " Philosophy of the human mind," in which he acknowledged in Descartes the master and initiator of modern philosophy. Samuel Miller's appreciation of Descartes is worth reproducing *in toto*, inasmuch as it may serve to explain the continuous popularity of the discourse *De Methodo* in American colleges during the eighteenth century:

> Descartes was the first metaphysician who drew a plain and intelligible line of distinction between the *intellectual* and the *material* world, or between *spirit* and *body*. The importance and utility of this distinction is obvious. He was the first who showed that the analogical mode of reasoning, concerning the powers of the mind, from the properties of the body is totally erroneous; and that accurate reflection on the operations of our mind, is the only way to gain a just knowledge of them. It was his philosophy which threw the *phantasms*, the *sensible species*, the *substantial forms*, &c. of the old system into disgrace, and introduced a more simple, perspicuous and rational method of investigating metaphysical truth. (II, 4, n.)

Miller's admiration for Locke's *Essay on Human Understanding* is unreserved, for this great work forms an "era in the history of metaphysical science." But while granting generously that Malebranche was "an acute and learned metaphysician," and that George Berkeley was "equally distinguished for the penetration and comprehensiveness of his mind, and the eminence of his virtues," he maintains that both of them "espoused a doctrine contrary to all our feelings and senses." Hume, Hartley, Reid, and Monboddo are worth mentioning "among the curiosities of the age" and the latter talks "with a semblance of reason and may be read with patience." Such is not the case of the celebrated Immanuel Kant, inventor of a system which has found great favor in Germany. Unable to understand a word in the general drift of Kant's system, Samuel Miller reproduced word for word a brief account of the Kantian philosophy published in a "British literary journal," adding as a footnote that, "The complaint that all this is obscure and scarcely intelligible will probably be made by every reader."

Of all the eighteenth century philosophers only one deserves unreserved admiration and endorsement, "the celebrated Ameri-

can divine, Mr. Jonathan Edwards, for some time President of
the College of New Jersey ":

> This gentlemen wrote on the side of moral *necessity*, or
> against the self-determining power of the will; and investi-
> gated the subject with a degree of originality, acuteness,
> depth, precision, and force of argument, which the accurate
> reader cannot contemplate but with astonishment. . . . It
> is worthy of remark, that our great countryman, Mr.
> Edwards, appears to have been the first *Calvinist* who
> avowed his belief so fully and thoroughly in the doctrine
> of moral necessity as his book indicates. Though all Cal-
> vinistic writers before his time were characterized by a firm
> adherence to the doctrine of *Predestination*; yet they seem,
> for the most part, to have adopted a kind of middle course
> between his creed and that of the Arminian *contingency*.
> The penetrating and comprehensive mind of Edwards went
> further; demonstrated that this middle ground was unten-
> able, and presented a more clear and satisfactory view of
> the doctrine of free grace, when contemplated through the
> medium of his main doctrine, than had ever before been
> given. (II, 30-31)

This very rapid and incomplete review of Samuel Miller's
opinions of the contemporary philosophers may help us to understand his attitude towards a group of French writers against
whom he pronounced a drastic condemnation. On this occasion, the author of the *Brief Retrospect* emphasized the necessary distinction, too often overlooked by historians, between
progress and *perfectibility*. This distinction becomes absolutely
essential in any study covering the latter half of the eighteenth
century. It was lost sight of during the battle which raged
around Diderot's *Encyclopédie*; it would help to explain both
the thesis defended by Jean-Jacques Rousseau in his *First Discourse* and the arguments of his opponents. Particularly it would
make more intelligible the attitude of American divines, like

John Witherspoon, whose admiration for material progress might otherwise be represented as a concession to the spirit of the Enlightenment. Samuel Miller's lengthy argumentation against the French advocates of the doctrine of perfectibility has at least the merit of stating unequivocally the position of the two enemy camps. It demonstrates at least that it was possible to keep within the orthodox Calvinistic fold while enjoying all the benefits and pleasantness of material progress:

> In the latter half of the century under consideration, a new doctrine concerning the human mind was announced, which is entitled to some notice in this place. This doctrine, it is believed, was first adopted and advanced by M. Helvetius, a celebrated French writer. He was followed by Mr. Condorcet, and some others also in France; by means of whose writings it obtained considerable currency among the literati of that country, and was afterwards embraced and defended, with much plausibility by Mr. Godwin, and others in Great-Britain.

In treating that momentous question Miller did not judge from second-hand information. He quoted and had probably read: Helvétius's *A Treatise on Man, his Intellectual Faculties, and his Education* (Translated by Hooper, 2 vols., 1777) ; and Condorcet's *Outline of an Historical View of the Progress of the Human Mind* (1795) ; Godwin's *Inquiry concerning Political Justice* (second edition, 2 vols., 1796). Intent upon preserving a judicial attitude, he specified that "It is not meant to be asserted that all these writers agree with respect to the details of their several systems; but that they concur in asserting the *omnipotence of education*, and the *perfectibility of man*." Before engaging in what was only a preliminary skirmish, Miller endeavored to reconnoiter the positions of the enemy:

> The advocates of this doctrine maintain the *Perfectibility*

of Man. With regard to the nature of the human mind they appear, in general, to embrace the system of *materialism.* They suppose that the thinking principle of man is the result of corporeal organization; that the difference in minds results from the difference in this organization, and more especially from the subsequent circumstances and education of the individual, that by means of the diffusion of knowledge, and the adoption of better principles and modes of education, the improvement of man in intellect, in virtue, and in happiness, will go on to an illimitable extent, that, at length, mind shall become "omnipotent over matter," perfect enjoyment assume the place of present suffering, and human life, instead of being bounded by a few years, be protracted to immortality, or at least to an indefinite duration.

Unfurling the banner of orthodoxy the theologian then entered the fray. But, even in the heat of the fight, Miller never indulged in the vituperations and anathema launched at that time by many of his brethren against the infidel philosophers. His condemnation is a summing up of the case, not the fierce denunciation of a pamphleteer:

> This system is unsupported by any facts; it is contrary to all the experience of mankind, it is opposed to every principle of human nature, and it is scarcely necessary to add, to the plainest dictates of Revelation. That man may, and probably will, make great improvements hereafter, in science and art, is readily admitted. That he cannot presume to assign the bounds to this improvement is also admitted. But that there will be absolutely no bounds to it, or, which is the same thing as to the argument, that it will go on beyond all assignable or conceivable limits, is to suppose the constitution of man essentially changed, his present wants, habits, and mode of subsistence totally superseded and a nature conferred upon him wholly different from that which his Creator gave him. (II, 29)

Samuel Miller intended to set forth his views more fully in the latter part of his work, and to show " the extravagance, weakness, inconsistency and injurious consequences " of the doctrine of perfectibility " with respect to its moral and political applications." So baneful and so widespread, however, was already the influence of the new system, that he could not wait for the uncertain publication of the last two parts of the *Brief Retrospect*. When he wrote his chapter on Education he felt that the doctrine of perfectibility was " too remarkable and too pregnant with mischief to be suffered to pass without more particular attention."

> It is, that Education has a kind of intellectual and moral *omnipotence*; that to its different forms are to be ascribed the chief, if not all the differences observable in the genius, talents and dispositions of men, and that by improving its principles and plan, human nature may, and finally will, reach a state of unlimited perfection in this world, or at least go on to a state of unlimited improvement. In short, in the estimation of those who adopt this doctrine, man is the child of circumstances; and by meliorating these, without the aid of religion, his true and highest elevation is to be obtained; and they even go so far as to believe that, by means of the advancement of light and knowledge, all vice, misery and death may finally be banished from the earth. This system, as before observed, seems to have been first distinctly taught by M. Helvetius, a celebrated French author, who wrote about the middle of the age we are considering, and was afterwards adopted and urged with great zeal by many of his countrymen, particularly Mirabaud, and Condorcet; and also by Mr. Godwin, and others, in Great Britain. (II, 292)

The condemnation of perfectibility is pronounced on four counts. First, it is contrary to the nature and condition of man—that is to say, to what may be called the doctrine of Christian individualism. This is an opportunity for Samuel Miller to emphasize, even more than he had done before, the necessary distinction between progress and perfectibility:

Though every succeeding generation may be said, with respect to literary and scientific acquisitions, to stand on the ground gained by their predecessors, and thus to be continually making progress; yet this is by no means the case with regard to intellectual discipline and moral qualities. Each successive individual, however elated the genius, and however sublime the virtues of his ancestors, has to perform the task of restraining his own appetites, subduing his own passions; and guarding against the excesses to which his irregular propensities would prompt him. . . . If every successive individual of our species must come into the world ignorant and feeble, and helpless; and if the same process for instilling knowledge into the mind, and restraining moral irregularities, must be undergone, *de novo*, in every instance, on what do these sanguine calculators rest their hopes that we shall attain a state of intellectual and moral perfection in the present world?

There we have, in clear and simple terms, one of the first definitions of that American individualism resting on a solid religious basis which was to be described so vividly by Tocqueville some thirty years later.

Miller's second objection to the doctrine of perfectibility is that it is "contrary to all experience." The world has existed for six thousand years; it may be granted that mankind is more enlightened than at any other period, but could we say that "real wisdom, moral purity and true happiness have always kept pace with the improvements in literature and the sciences? Are the most learned and scientific nations and the most learned and scientific individuals, always the most virtuous? Are luxury, fraud, violence, unprincipled ambition, the vicious intercourse of the sexes, and the various kinds of intemperance less frequent among the polished and enlightened nations of Europe than among the untutored natives of America? "

We might easily infer from this quotation that Miller had intended to give an answer to the famous question proposed by the Académie de Dijon and treated by Jean-Jacques Rousseau in his *Discours sur les sciences et les arts*. But Miller's reasoning is entirely different from the demonstration of the philosopher from Geneva. In fact he would deny that there was any problem at all. If the principle that knowledge alone is sufficient to reform, exalt and finally render perfect the human race, " we should find virtue and happiness both in individuals and societies, bearing an exact proportion to the advances made in knowledge. . . . But if it not be *generally* true, that in proportion as men make progress in intellectual improvement, they make progress in moral excellence; we may with confidence conclude, that these two species of improvement do not necessarily stand in relation of cause and effect to each other, and therefore that from the existence of the former we cannot legitimately infer the existence of the latter."

This is a far cry from the denunciation of society and civilization in the famous *Discours* of Rousseau, but perfectly consistent with his refusal to admit that education or circumstances alone can modify or condition the moral behavior of man. It is also consistent with the attitude observed by Miller all through the *Brief Retrospect*, in maintaining that the scientific, artistic, or literary achievements of a given man are completely independent of his religious beliefs.

His third argument is a striking illustration of the necessity of differentiating between what is too commonly called progress and " melioration." Increase in population was generally considered as a progress in the eighteenth century, but it has been asserted " by acute and well informed writers, that the progress of population, when unrestrained, is always in a geometrical ratio, and that the increase of the means of subsistence is, under the most favourable circumstances, only in an arithmetical ratio." This is clearly a case when a so-called progress results almost necessarily in unmitigated evil. This argument did not apply evidently to conditions then existing in America, but would ultimately apply to any country afflicted with an indefinite increase of population. Needless to say here that Samuel Miller could not claim any credit for these pessimistic considerations. He had borrowed them from " an anonymous work," recently published under the title *An Essay on Population*, " a work which, in force of reasoning, and in candour and urbanity of discussion, has rarely if ever been exceeded." In Malthus's *Essay* Samuel Miller had found a cold-blooded and " scientific" refutation of the visions of Godwin and Condorcet and particularly of " the perfectibility of man and society ":

> . . . It is evident, that the progress of population must continually, unless in extraordinary circumstances, be checked by the want of subsistence; that these two will ever be, from their very nature, contending forces, and will be found more or less, in the most advantageous states of society, to produce want, fraud, violence, irregularity in sexual intercourse, disease, and various kinds of vice; and, as the natural consequence of these, especially in their combined force, much misery and degradation to man. There seems to be no method of avoiding this conclusion, but by contending, that when knowledge shall have made a certain degree of progress, both the intercourse of the sexes, and the necessity of food and raiment will cease. But will any one seriously maintain that such events are probable? Do we actually see individuals or communities, as they advance in learning and refinement, discover less propensity to the sexual intercourse, or a greater disposition or ability to do without the means of bodily sustenance? It will not be pretended that either of these is the case. But as long as the

propagation of the human species continues to stand on the footing and to depend on the principles which it now does; and as long as food and raiment are necessary as means of subsistence, human society must be doomed to exhibit more or less of ignorance, vice, and misery.

In his fourth and final argument, Samuel Miller contrasts the Millenium of the philosophers and the Millenium of the Bible:

The sacred volume teaches us that we are fallen and depraved beings; that this depravity is total, and admits no remedy but by the grace declared in the Gospel; that the most virtuous will never be perfect or completely holy in the present world, and that misery and death are the unavoidable lot of man under the present dispensation.

It is true that the Scriptures speak of a millenium or period of happiness, but the Millenium of the Bible differs essentially both in cause and nature from the Millenium depicted in philosophic dreams, which is only " an absurd portrait of knowledge without real wisdom, of benevolence without piety, and of purity and happiness without genuine virtue."

In conclusion, Miller is willing to grant that education is extremely powerful; that much of the difference we observe in the talents and dispositions of men is to be ascribed to its efficacy; and that " the lovers of knowledge may be expected hereafter to make such improvements in literature, such discoveries in science, and such useful reforms in the plans of instruction, as exceedingly to promote the general improvement of man." Unfortunately although the eighteenth century has witnessed important " revolutions " in education, it cannot be said that they constituted real improvements: " Particularly with respect to the patient, laborious and thorough investigation of the various objects of knowledge, the depth of erudition; the discipline and subordination of academic establishments; and the general moral influence of literary and scientific acquirements, the last age cannot with propriety boast of much progress." (II, 302)

Samuel Miller realized how incomplete and rapid was his characterization of the eighteenth century, since he had to postpone dealing with the fundamental subjects of politics, morals and religion. He undertook, nevertheless, to sum up in a final chapter, entitled *Recapitulation*, the various aspects of the period as far as they had been presented in the *Brief Retrospect*. All considered, it could be asserted with confidence "that in no period of the same extent, since the creation, has a mass of improvement so large, diversified and rich been presented to view." "No less than fifteen characteristics could be found, some good, some bad, and every one of them susceptible of qualifications and reservations. We shall try to give them here in Samuel Miller's own words, while regretting not to be able to reproduce in full the text of our author. According to him, the eighteenth century was:

(1) An age of free inquiry; (2) the age of physical science; (3) the age of economical science, marked by a real revolution in medicine and in all subjects pertaining to the welfare of man; (4) the age of experiment, under the influence of Bacon; (5) the age of revolutions in science, brought about by the rapid succession of discoveries, hypotheses and systems; (6) the age of printing, with a prodigious increase of new works and new editions of old works; (7) the age of books, the spirit of writing exceeding all former precedents, and resulting in hasty productions of books and periodicals; (8) the age of unprecedented diffusion of knowledge, for common people read and inquired to a degree that would have been thought incredible in an earlier century, while seminaries of learning and circulating libraries were multiplied; (9) the age of superficial learning, ("the unprecedented circulation of magazines, literary

journals, Abridgments, Epitomes, &c., with which the republic of letters has been deluged, particularly within the last forty years. These have distracted the attention of the student, have seduced him from sources of more systematic and comprehensive instruction, and have puffed up multitudes with false ideas of their own acquirements "); (10) the age of taste and refinement; (11) the age of infidel philosophy, which has poisoned the principles and completed the ruin of millions; (12) and yet the age of Christian Science, for a better knowledge of the universe and of the history of man should lead us to a greater admiration for the work of the Creator; (13) the age of translations, which have established closer contacts between different peoples; (14) the age of literary honours, and of international memberships in learned societies, and (15) the age of literary and scientific intercourse, for while in all preceding ages literary men were in a great measure " insulated," increased facilities in transportation have enabled them to travel and to communicate freely. Taking all in all, it could be asserted that great as were the achievements of the age just come to a close, they only heralded the opening of a still greater era and " that substantial advancement in knowledge which the enlightened and benevolent mind anticipates with a glow of delight."

This analysis of the most important problem treated in the Brief Retrospect is far too sketchy and incomplete to justify any formal conclusion. A comparison with Miller's immediate predecessors and contemporaries cannot easily be made, since he has not dealt with the most controversial aspects of the doctrine of progress, namely politics, morals and religion. He has said enough, however, to enable us to determine the distinctive features and the main lines of his approach.

The most striking is the sharp distinction established between progress and perfectibility. The word progress itself does not necessarily imply improvement, but change, slow and gradual, or sudden and revolutionary, for the better or for the worse, according to the circumstances and the use that man makes of his discoveries. These discoveries have a cumulative effect and pass on from one generation to another. But limits have been assigned by the Creator to the power of man's intellect. These limits are unknown and there are still worlds to conquer, but sooner or later they will be reached. However great may be the knowledge of man, knowledge will never make him complete master of natural forces. Finally there is practically no relation between scientific knowledge, artistic and literary achievements and morality, virtue and true happiness.

In the domain of morality, virtue, religion and to a certain extent of the intellect, on the contrary, everyman starts *de novo*. He is born feeble physically and mentally. He has to fight the same fight as his forebears, to overcome the same obstacles, to repress the same instincts or impulses, to check the evil tendencies which are in him. He may encounter circumstances more or less favorable and it is granted that education and particularly religious education may help him, but in the last analysis every individual stands on his own and remains a weak, imperfect and sinful creature, but for the grace of God.

Of course this is straight Calvinism and we know that Samuel Miller was uncompromisingly orthodox in his religious tenets, but in fact he was much closer to Saint Augustine than to Calvin. An examination of the last chapters of the *City of God* (Book XXII, Ch. 24 and 29) would provide a most fitting commentary to the conclusion of the *Brief Retrospect*. There one will find a triumphal hymn to human industry, extending to all the realms of human activities: " Vestimentorum et aedificiorum ad opera quam mirabilia, quam stupenda, industria humana pervenerit; quo in agricultura, quo in navigatione profecerit; quae in fabricatione quoque vasorum, vel etiam statuarum et picturarum

varietate excogitavit." Nothing new under the sun—improvements in the daily life of every man, in his clothes, in housing,
farming and navigation, in domestic utensils and in works of
art, all the modern comforts and enjoyments, so highly praised
by Samuel Miller and by him presented as conquests of the
eighteenth century—were already the privilege of Saint Augustine's contemporaries. The conclusion is strikingly similar for,
according to Augustine, however extensive may be the discoveries
of man and the apparent happiness prevailing in the terrestrial
city, perfection can never be attained, since " in the torrent which
carries mankind along the evil which they received from their
progenitor and the good which was granted by the Creator are
inextricably mixed: utrumque simul currit isto quasi fluvio
atque torrente generis humani, malum quod a parente trahitur,
et bonum quod a creante tribuitur."

Whether the distinction established by Samuel Miller between
progress and perfectibility was observed by many of his American contemporaries, I am not prepared to say. We know that
Franklin at least on one occasion had deplored the fact that
morality and science did not proceed *pari passu*. After con-
gratulating Priestley on his new experiments " on the purification
of the atmosphere by means of vegetation " the old doctor added:

> The rapid Progress *true* Science now makes, occasions my
> regretting that I was born so soon. It is impossible to
> imagine the Height to which may be carried, in a thousand
> years, the Power of Man over Matter. We may perhaps
> learn to deprive large Masses of their Gravity, and give
> them absolute Levity, for the sake of easy Transport. Agri-
> culture may diminish its Labour and double its Produce;
> all Diseases may by sure means be prevented or cured, not
> excepting even that of old Age, and our Lives lengthened
> at pleasure even beyond the antediluvian Standard. O that
> moral Science were in as fair a way of Improvement, that
> Men would cease to be Wolves to one another, and that

human Beings would at length learn what they now improperly call Humanity. (Passy, Feb. 8, 1780, Smyth ed. VIII, 9)

Seventeen years later, in one of his not so rare moments of despondency, Thomas Jefferson wrote to Bishop Madison: " What is called civilization seems to have no other effect on him [man] than to teach him to pursue the principle of *bellum omnium in omnia* on a larger scale, and in place of the little contests of tribe against tribe, to engage all the quarters of the earth in the same work of destruction." (Jan. 1, 1797. *Memorial ed.*, IX, 359-60.)

But both Franklin and Jefferson were fundamentally in harmony with the *philosophes*. They observed and deplored the lag existing between scientific discoveries and social progress and their Americanism was too strong to permit them to indulge for long in pessimistic considerations. We have to turn to France to find a parallel to the fight waged by Samuel Miller against the upholders of the doctrine of perfectibility. Without going into the antecedents of the movement, let us simply recall that Madame de Staël had published the first edition of her famous work *De la littérature considérée dans ses rapports avec les institutions sociales* in 1800, and that, in 1802, there appeared a second edition, revised, with a long preface in which she attempted, not very successfully, to distinguish between progress and perfectibility. It was, according to her, the problem of the age: " D'où vient donc que ce système de la perfectibilité de l'espèce humaine déchaîne maintenant toutes les passions politiques? " It was the fundamental problem discussed by Chateaubriand not only in his *Lettre à M. de Fontanes sur la seconde édition de l'ouvrage de Madame de Staël*, but also in the *Génie du Christianisme* which preceded the *Brief Retrospect* less than two years (April, 1802) . Shall we recall that Chateaubriand gave a whole chapter to the study of the "Constitution primitive de l'homme. Nouvelle preuve du péché originel" (Première partie, Livre III, Ch. 2)? That in the book devoted to the progress of the sciences, particularly Astronomy and Mathematics, Chateaubriand endeavoured to define the limits of human knowledge? That in the *Essai sur les Révolutions* he had already taken sides, in addressing those who are dazzled by "le système de la perfection"? Whatever may be the shortcomings of the hasty production of Samuel Miller, the forgotten book of a forgotten man, and however incomplete is this altogether too brief account of it, we hope at least to have shown that the *Brief Retrospect* was a not altogether negligible contribution to the great debate, still going on in our days on the extent and limitations of human knowledge.

BIO-BIBLIOGRAPHICAL NOTE

There is no adequate biography of Samuel Miller. *The Life of Samuel Miller*, by his son Samuel Miller (Philadelphia, 2 vols., 1869) remains the principal source of information. See also the *Genealogical and Personal Memorial of Mercer County*, edited by Francis Bazley Lee, Vol. I, p. 267 ff. (New York and Chicago, 1907) ; John De Witt, "Intellectual Life of Samuel Miller," in *Princeton Theological Review* (April, 1906) ; and my article on " A Landmark in American Intellectual History," *The Princeton University Library Chronicle*, Vol. XIV, No. 2 (Winter, 1953). Professor Harold S. Jantz has written an excellent article on Samuel Miller's "Survey of German Literature, 1803)," *The Germanic Review*, Vol. XIV, No. 4 (Dec., 1941), followed by a description of "The Samuel Miller Papers at Princeton," *The Princeton University Library Chronicle*, Vol. IV, Nos. 2 and 3 (Feb.-April, 1943). The libraries of Princeton University and of the Princeton Theological Seminary possess good collections of the writings of Miller and very important manuscripts, including in addition to a very large correspondence a file listed as " Papers for the second edition of part I of the Retrospect," a " List of my publications, 1793–1836 " established by Miller himself.

A bibliography of studies of the idea of progress would be endless and would include a large part of the work done by Lovejoy. I shall mention here, almost at random, only a few titles such as Lois Whitney, *Primitivism and the Idea of Progress in English Popular Literature of the Eighteenth Century* (Baltimore, 1934) ; Howard Mumford Jones, *Ideas in America* (Cambridge, 1944) ; Ronald S. Crane, " Anglican Apologetics and the Idea of Progress, 1699-1745," *Modern Philology*, Vol. XXXII, Nos. 3 and 4 (Feb. and May, 1934) ; Rutherford E. Delmage, " The American Idea of Progress, 1750–1800," *Proceedings of the American Philosophical Society*, Vol. 91, No. 4 (October, 1947) ; Theodor E. Mommsen, " St. Augustine and the Christian Idea of Progress," *Journal of the History of Ideas*, Vol. XII, No. 3 (June, 1951) ; Robert E. Palmer, *Catholics and Unbelievers in Eighteenth Century France* (Princeton, 1939) ; Gladys Bryson, *Man and Society: The Scottish Inquiry of the Eighteenth Century* (Princeton, 1948) ; and Adolf Koch, *Republic Religion* (New York, 1933). With the exception of Robert E. Palmer, however, the authors of these studies do not seem to have emphasized the distinction between progress and perfectibility—many of them use either term indifferently or list them together.

OWSEI TEMKIN

An Historical Analysis of the Concept of Infection *

⋙⋙⋙⋙⋙⋙⋙⋙⋙⋙⋙⋙

The most recent edition of one of our standard medical dictionaries defines "infection" as follows: "Invasion of the tissues of the body by pathogenic organisms in such a way that injury followed by reactive phenomena results." [1] This definition shows the earmarks of modern medical research. It is only since about 1800, the days of Bichat, that we have become accustomed to speak of the tissues of the body. The words "pathogenic organisms" remind us of the rise of bacteriology. Obviously, a definition of infection like the above could hardly have been formulated before the days of Pasteur, Koch, and Lister. And the qualification that the presence of pathogenic organisms, though necessary,

---

* In partly different form and under different title, this article was originally presented as a paper before the Sigma Xi Society, in Ithaca, N. Y., in 1952. Because of the great role of infection in medicine, the article is, by necessity, incomplete as to historical details and literature quoted. The following works may be cited as supplementing some of its omissions: C. E. A. Winslow, *The Conquest of Epidemic Disease,* Princeton University Press, 1943; Richard H. Shryock, *The Development of Modern Medicine,* New York, Knopf, 1947; John E. Gordon, Evolution of an Epidemiology of Health, in *The Epidemiology of Health,* Iago Galdston, editor, New York-Minneapolis, Health Education Council, 1953; also Vilmos Manninger, *Der Entwickelungsgang der Antiseptik und Aseptik,* Breslau, 1904 (Abhandlungen zur Geschichte der Medicin, Heft XII).

[1] *The American Illustrated Medical Dictionary.* Twenty-second edition, Philadelphia, W. B. Saunders Co., 1951, p. 738.

123

is not sufficient, that injury followed by reactive phenomena must have resulted, points to an even more recent date. In short, the above definition of infection seems to be scientifically accurate, consisting, as it does, mainly of terms which bear a well defined connotation verifiable by observation. I say *mainly*, because here, as elsewhere in medicine, there remains an element of more doubtful character. What exactly is an " injury," and what is an " invasion " ? We shall come back to these disturbing elements in the definition. For the moment let us be content with the fact that the modern concept of infection is reasonably clear and that it is couched in the language of modern science.

This being the case, we may be all the more permitted to wonder at the incongruity between the definition and the term defined. The word " infection," as well as its counterparts in other languages, is much older than the nineteenth century. I need hardly point out that infection is derived from the Latin *infectio*. Now, one may easily say that there is nothing unusual in an old term receiving a more precise explanation with the advance of science. People talked about " fever " long before they knew how to measure the temperature of the body, and of " pneumonia " before any post mortem dissections had been performed on human bodies. Infection must have occurred at all times; the word expresses a phenomenon that has remained the same, although its scientific explanation was reserved for a more advanced age. Encouraged by this thought, we turn to ancient medical literature and we find indeed that Theodorus Priscianus, a physician of the fifth century A. D., devotes a whole chapter to " *infectio* " in his textbook of medicine. However, the chapter is entitled: *De infectionibus capillorum*,[2] i. e., " On the dyeing of hair." We shall have to admit, I think, that the

---

[2] Theodorus Priscianus *Euporiston libri III*, ed. Valentine Rose, Lipsiae, 1894, I, c. 2, p. 5 ff.

matter is not quite as simple as we assumed. The word included a connotation which it no longer possesses today.

There is no other way but to inquire more closely into the meaning of those words which have come to be used for the concept of infection. The Latin "*infectio*," as we just heard, means staining or dyeing. And to stain or to color is one of the principal connotations of the verb "*inficere*." The root meaning of this word is to put or dip into something, and the something may be a dye; or to mix with something, especially a poison; or to stain something in the sense that it becomes tainted, spoiled, or corrupted. Indeed, the English word "to stain" can still be used in the double sense of dyeing as well as polluting. Let us remember, then, that an infection is basically a pollution. And the same is true of the term "contagion" which indicates a pollution, especially by direct contact. Peculiarly enough, the Greek verb *miaino* presents a counterpart to the Latin *inficere*. Here too the mere staining can be included together with physical or moral defiling. And the corresponding noun "*miasma*" originally meant any pollution or polluting agent.

This brief linguistic excursion will suffice to bring out a basic element in the concept of infection: impurity. If we look for examples we have only to turn to chapter 13 of Leviticus which deals with Zara'ath, the disease commonly translated as leprosy. "And the leper in whom the plague is, his clothes shall be rent, and his head bare, and he shall put a covering upon his upper lip, and shall cry, Unclean, unclean. All the days wherein the plague shall be in him he shall be defiled; he is unclean; he shall dwell alone; without the camp shall his habitation be" (ch. 13, vs. 45 and 46). The leper is obviously isolated so that he may not communicate his uncleanness; for persons, animals, and things unclean make those who come in contact with them unclean too. This, according to the Bible, holds true of men suffering from gonorrhea, and of men and women in the sphere of sexual functions; it holds true of the beasts that are unclean and forbidden food; and it also holds true of dead objects.

The chapter dealing with Zara'ath greatly influenced the medieval attitude towards leprosy and the segregation of lepers. The contagiousness of leprosy was dreaded beyond the real danger of infection. Nevertheless, this attitude may have helped to make those countries where regulations were rigorously enforced almost free of leprosy around 1600. No wonder that the sanitary significance of Leviticus has been greatly praised, especially since washing of clothes and bathing in water were mandatory in the process of purification! [3] It is not necessary to deny that, as far as leprosy, gonorrhea, and the eating of carrion flesh are concerned, an empirical insight into the real danger existed. But the guiding thought was that of a ritualistic religious taboo. " Thus shall ye separate the children of Israel from their uncleanness; that they die not in their uncleanness, when they defile my tabernacle that is among them." [4] The diseases mentioned as unclean in Leviticus are but one type of pollution among others.[5] We are not even quite certain exactly what disease Zara'ath was. Even if it included what we now call leprosy,[6] it must have included other conditions as well. The sufferer from Zara'ath might recover and be cleansed from his impurity. On the other hand, even garments and houses could be affected by Zara'ath.

According to an age-old belief, disease could be sent by the gods as punishment for a crime with which men had defiled

[3] Leviticus, ch. 14, v. 8.

[4] Leviticus, ch. 15, v. 31.

[5] Wolf von Siebenthal, *Krankheit als Folge der Sünde,* Hannover, 1950, passim, has shown a similar relationship in other civilizations between disease and pollution.

[6] This has been doubted by F. C. Lendrum, *J. A. M. A.*, 1952, vol. 148, p. 222.

themselves. The Bible mentions leprosy as well as plague as instances. According to the Greeks, Apollo shot his plague arrows upon the Greek host before Troy because their leader, Agamemnon, had abducted the daughter of his priest. The girl had to be returned. "And," as Homer tells us, " they purified themselves, and cast the defilement into the sea, and offered to Apollo acceptable hecatombs of bulls and goats by the shore of the unresting sea." [7] Likewise, Apollo sent the plague upon Thebes because Oedipus, the King, had killed his father and married his mother, so that a pollution, a miasma, infested the land.[8] The ideas of a disease caused by a foul deed, and of a disease defiling the sufferer, were almost interchangeable.

Around 400 B. C., a Greek physician wrote a book " On the Sacred Disease," the popular name for epilepsy, in which he attacked the popular healers. " For the sufferers from the disease they purify with blood and such like, as though they were polluted, bloodguilty, bewitched by men, or had committed some unholy act." But to the belief that gods or demons might cause the disease, our author opposes his own enlightened view: " However, I hold that a man's body is not defiled by a god, the one being utterly corrupt the other perfectly holy. Nay, even should it have been defiled or in any way injured through some different agency, a god is more likely to purify and sanctify it than he is to cause defilement." [9] This opposition of a natural explanation of disease to the religious or magic one which is expressed in the so-called Hippocratic writings is of great import for the concept

---

[7] Homer, *Iliad*, I, 314-316. Translation by A. T. Murray, Loeb Classical Library, I, p. 27. E. R. Dodds, *The Greeks and the Irrational*, Berkeley, 1951, p. 36, claims that the belief in pollution as infectious was post-Homeric; see, however, my review in *Isis*, 1952, vol. 43, p. 375 f.

[8] Sophocles, *Oedipus the King*, 96-98.

[9] *Hippocrates*, with an English translation by H. W. S. Jones, Loeb Classical Library, II, p. 149.

of infection. Speculating on the significance of air, another Hippocratic author reasons that pestilences or epidemic fevers must be due to the air that all men inhale at the same time. "So whenever the air has been tainted with such pollutions (*miasmasin*) as are hostile to the human race, then men fall sick . . . ." [10] Keeping within the old terminology of miasma, a secularization has been achieved. The plague is no longer considered a punishment for religious or moral defilement; instead it has become the result of a defilement of the air, due to some mysterious agents suspended in it. The transmutation is not even so startling as we might think at first. In the myths it is the sun god Apollo that sends pestilences, now it is still the sky—especially the sun—that acts upon the air. "Why is it that when considerable vapor arises under the action of the sun, the year is inclined to plague?" asks a somewhat later philosopher.[11] We have it on good ancient authority that the forecasting of "droughts and rainstorms and plagues and earthquakes and other changes in the surrounding vault of a similar character" was considered a serious part of astronomy not on a par with the casting of nativities.[12]

Medicine from Antiquity to the Renaissance is replete with references to planets and conjunctions that breed pestilences and new diseases. The name for "influenza" is derived from the influence of the stars. But there is also intermingled a good deal of climatology that may be wrong but not dependent upon ideas

[10] *Ibid.*, p. 235. I have substituted "tainted" where Jones has "infected."

[11] Pseudo-Aristotle, *Problems*, I, 21. Translation by W. S. Hett, Loeb Classical Library, I, p. 19. According to a late Greek source (Clemens Alexandrinus) the Egyptians too derived epidemics from the sun; see Theodor Puschmann, *Die Geschichte der Lehre von der Ansteckung*, Wien, 1895, p. 4.

[12] Sextus Empiricus, *Against the Professors*, V, 2. Translation by R. G. Bury, Loeb Classical Library, IV, p. 323. On Aristotle's theory, e. g. to explain evaporations and earthquakes by action of the sun, cf. Otto Gilbert, *Die meteorologischen Theorien des griechischen Altertums*, Leipzig, 1907, p. 307.

of universal sympathy and astral spirits. At any rate the notion that epidemic diseases were connected with weather and winds, seasons, floods, and earthquakes remained firmly established until the second half of the nineteenth century. Here again it is hard to say where actual experience of the seasonal prevalence of such diseases as infantile paralysis, malarial fevers, upper respiratory infections, diarrhea of infants, and others ended and where meteorological speculation, which saw in epidemics a telluric event of divine or cosmic origin, began.

II

Although all diseases could conceivably be judged as punishment for crime, it appears that there existed a popular classification of diseases into clean and unclean, the latter being " infections " par excellence. Of these latter, we mentioned leprosy, gonorrhea, plague, and epilepsy, to which insanity might be added. In the popular mind these types of diseases had and have a moral or religious stigma. The plague as God's wrath at a sinful people, leprosy and venereal disease as filthy, mental disease as a disgrace, are notions very much alive even today. In former times these diseases were popularly considered not only as pollutions but also as possibly catching. The super-stitious Greek or Roman spit when he met insane or epileptic persons, and people were afraid to eat or drink from a dish an epileptic had used. The pressure of opinion seems to have induced medieval physicians to uphold this belief, at the same time rationalizing it by a natural explanation. The breath of the epileptic was now accused of carrying the contagion. This explanation was ready-made since the ancients had ascribed such a role to the breath in other diseases, e. g., consumption.

Only in the sixteenth century was the fable of the contagiousness of epilepsy definitely eliminated from the medical literature.[13]

Although the occurrence of contagion among men and animals was known to the ancients, they did not elaborate the concept systematically.[14] It is still one of the great puzzles of historical pathology that such infections as measles, scarlet fever, and smallpox are not recorded in classical literature. Did they not exist, or were they not conceived as specific diseases? Whatever the answer may be, the fact remains that the first systematic enumeration of contagious diseases is to be found in the so-called *Book of Treasure*, an Arabic textbook of medicine, compiled not later than about 900 A. D. The author enumerates the following contagious diseases: " Leprosy, scabies, small-pox, measles, ozaena, ophthalmia and the pestilential diseases." [15] To this list we may add a Latin one, dating from the thirteenth century, naming acute fever, consumption, epilepsy, scabies, ignis sacer, anthrax, ophthalmia, and leprosy.[16] These lists show a considerable knowledge of " contagious diseases, that is those which infect others," as they were called,[17] although their nosological interpretation is not easy. Karl Sudhoff explained the " acute fever " as plague or typhus, and " ignis sacer " as erysipelas,

---

[13] See O. Temkin, *The Falling Sickness*, Baltimore, The Johns Hopkins Press, 1945, pp. 7 and 114 ff.

[14] See Puschmann, *Die Geschichte der Lehre von der Ansteckung*, Wien, 1895; Karl Sudhoff, Infektionsverhütung im Wandel der Zeiten und Anschauungen. Reprinted in *Arch. Gesch. Med.*, 1929, vol. 21, pp. 207-218. The concept of medical infection is clearly expressed in Thucydides' account of the plague, especially II, 51 where he uses the same verb " *anapimplemi* " that also carries the notion of " defiling."

[15] Max Meyerhof, The " Book of Treasure," an Early Arabic Treatise on Medicine, *Isis*, vol. 14, 1930, pp. 53-76, see p. 61.

[16] Karl Sudhoff, Die acht ansteckenden Krankheiten einer angeblichen Baseler Ratsverordnung vom Jahre 1400. Reprinted in *Arch. Gesch. Med.*, vol. 21, 1929, pp. 219-227, see p. 224 f.

[17] *Ibid.*, p. 227: " *Hii sunt morbi contagiosi, id est inficientes alios. . . .*"

although ergotism is just as likely an interpretation. Sudhoff was obviously guided by the idea that these diseases should be infectious from our point of view. The naming of ozaena in the Arabic list, together with epilepsy in the Latin one, shows how misleading this may be. Ozaena is a condition characterized by a foul discharge from the nose. Quite possibly it was the evil smell that led to the belief of contagiousness. Nevertheless, we may say that the clinical study of infectious diseases was well under way. By the middle of the sixteenth century, the nervous diseases had been eliminated from serious medical consideration, while syphilis, typhus, scarlet fever, and influenza had been added. The further development of this clinical knowledge is outside our theme. Instead we have to return to the theory of infection as pollution and the associations it evoked of something bad, to be avoided and if possible removed.

III

The statement that epidemic disease is caused by miasms, i. e., pollution of the air, in itself seems to have given the illusion of an explanation. This illusion was supported by the meaning of infection as staining. The analogy with a tincture where a small drop of dye-stuff suffices to color a large amount of fluid played an important role in medieval alchemy and medicine. It helped to explain how the whole body could become sick from mere contact or inhaled breath.[18] Finally, and perhaps most important, there was the decay and putrescence of organic bodies, "*sepsis*," to cite the Greek word which we still use. Putrescence became the pattern of pollution and the evil smell it propagated

---

[18] Aretaeus, VIII, 131, speaking of the communicability of elephantiasis (leprosy) refers at once to the "*baphe*" (in the sense of the Latin "infectio") and its transmission ("*metadosis*") by the breath.

was taken as an indication and guide. To quote an old English version of a medieval poem, the so-called School of Salerno:

> *Though all ill savours do not breed infection,*
> *Yet sure infection commeth most by smelling* [19]

The evil smell from the refuse of slaughter houses and from a sick person was supposed to cause infection, as was the unpleasant odor hovering over marshes, the malaria, bad air, of later days. The latter in particular was called "*virus*," a word that could also designate the poisonous secretion of snakes. A chain of associated words and images thus provided a theory of infection, and it is remarkable how our modern terminology has remained within the orbit of ancient and medieval imagery. Indeed, the fight against epidemic diseases was guided by very similar notions in the fourteenth century and in the middle of the nineteenth. In 1347 bubonic plague, the black death, began its devastating reign and stimulated the creation of public health measures in medieval towns in times of pestilence. The streets were cleaned, the keeping of pigs and the emptying of cesspools were forbidden. In England the first general statute against nuisances was enacted in 1388.[20] To cleanse the air, pyres were lighted in the streets, the rooms and beds were scented with vinegar and perfumes. Since evil smell caused sickness, a pleasant one would remove it.[21] Here we witness the fallacy of ascribing physical effects to what was pleasant, a confusion of science and aesthetics. Pyres disappeared in the eighteenth century when

---

[19] *The School of Salernum*, New York, Hoeber, 1920, p. 87.

[20] John Simon, *English Sanitary Institutions*, London, 1890, p. 41, note.

[21] The idea of fire and good odors combating the plague goes back to antiquity. Galen, Ad Pisonem de theriaca liber, c. 16 (ed. Kühn, vol. 14, p. 281) tells the story of Hippocrates who ordered the Athenians to have fires lighted throughout their city and to use the best smelling substances as fuel.

better means of ventilation were invented, but in many respects the great sanitary movement of the nineteenth century followed in the old medieval footsteps. It started in England in the 1830's under the impact of the asiatic cholera that had invaded Europe in 1831 and of the appalling morbidity and death rate of the working population herded into the cities by the industrial revolution. These people lived in squalor and filth, and the sanitarians directed their efforts against these conditions. This is what John Simon, one of the medical protagonists of public health, in 1874, had to say of the fatal influence of uncleanliness:

> . . . I do not refer to it in its minor degrees, as compared with high standards of cleanliness or chemical purity, but refer chiefly to such degrees of it as fall, or ought to fall, within the designation of FILTH:–to degrees, namely, which in most cases obviously, and in other cases under but slight mask, are such as any average man or woman should be disgusted at: such as, eminently, the presence of putrescent refuse-matter, solid and fluid, causing nuisance by its effluvia and soakage. Also in imputing to Filth, as thus illustrated, that its effluvia are largely productive of disease, I do not ignore that disease is also abundantly caused by air which is fouled in other ways.[22]

More briefly and poetically the same thought had been expressed in the following verses:

> *In houses where you mind to make your dwelling,*
> *That neere the same there be no evill sents*
> *Of puddle-waters, or of excrements,*
> *Let aire be cleere and light, and free from faults,*
> *That come of secret passages and vaults.*[23]

Today we distinguish between disinfectant and deodorant.

---

[22] John Simon, *Public Health Reports*, vol. 2, London, 1887, p. 450.
[23] *The School of Salernum*, op. cit., p. 87.

But as long as pollution of the air was a guiding concept, including any impurity noticeable to the senses or by its alleged results, such a distinction was almost impossible to make. In 1881, Littré's dictionary still defines " désinfection " as: "Action d'enlever à l'air, à un appartement, aux vêtements, aux divers tissus organiques, ou à un corps quelconque, les miasmes dangereux ou les odeurs désagréables qui les infectent." [24] It is, therefore, not astonishing to see that physicians and surgeons in using disinfectants or antiseptics largely relied on their deodorant effect. Thus Semmelweis, who in 1847 discovered that childbed fever was caused by " disintegrating organic material " carried by the attending obstetricians, prescribed disinfection of hands with chlorinated lime, guided by the deodorant action of this substance.[25]

As regards the scientific explanations of infection originating between the late Middle Ages and about 1850, they did not contribute much to a better understanding either, ingenious and interesting, nay even prophetic, as many isolated contributions were.

Limiting ourselves to a very brief survey, we find Fracastoro, in the sixteenth century, elaborating a theory of contagion that summarizes ancient and medieval experience; while Sydenham in the seventeenth century reformulates epidemiological doctrines.[26] According to Fracastoro, contagious diseases spread

[24] E. Littré, *Dictionnaire de la Langue Française*, T. 2, Paris, 1881, p. 1105.

[25] Ignaz Philipp Semmelweis, Die Aetiologie, der Begriff und die Prophylaxis des Kindbettfiebers, in *Gesammelte Werke,* ed. Tiberius von Györy, Jena, G. Fischer, 1905, p. 130: " Dass nach der gewöhnlichen Art des Waschens der Hände mit Seife die an der Hand klebenden Cadavertheile nicht sämmtlich entfernt werden, beweist der cadaveröse Geruch, welchen die Hand für längere oder kürzere Zeit behält."

[26] For details cf. C. E. A. Winslow, *op. cit.*

by a transfer of imperceptible particles *(seminaria)* [27] from an infected body to another by direct contact, via an intermediate object *(fomes)*, or at a distance.[28] While infection can originate in a sick body spontaneously, contagion accounts for the transmittal of the same disease to other bodies. Infection, primary as well as induced, is a form of putrescence.[29] The most original feature in Fracastoro's work, apart from his clinical differentiation of typhus and other diseases, is his insistence that the seeds of contagion are particles which can even propagate themselves in neighboring parts, and his differentiation of two kinds of putrefaction, one accompanied by " a stench and a disgusting taste " [30] and the other which may proceed without it like the change of wine into vinegar. These views are interesting regardless of whether Fracastoro really anticipated the fermentative, or enzymatic, action involved in infectious processes or merely realized that there were different ways for things to get spoiled.

Sydenham's interest, conforming with his intention to imitate Hippocrates and to describe diseases as they appeared and disappeared, centered on the epidemic constitution of years and seasons. It is not too great an exaggeration to say that the medical theory of infection around 1850 had not progressed considerably beyond these two men. For one thing it was very much confused. Infection was used synonymously with, or differently from, contagion. If distinguished, infection was attributed to agents consisting " almost entirely of decayed or diseased organized

[27] Hieronymus Fracastorius, *De contagione et contagiosis morbis et eorum curatione, libri III.* Translation and notes by C. Wright, New York, Putnam, 1930, book I, ch. 3, p. 10.

[28] *Ibid.*, ch. 2 ff.

[29] *Ibid.*, especially chs. 1, 3, and 9.

[30] *Ibid.*, ch. 9, p. 41. Although Fracastoro hardly believed in the organismic nature of these particles, such a view became widespread towards the end of the seventeenth century, see Manninger, *op. cit.*, p. 26 ff.

substances, and of animal emanations or secretions . . . found to exist most abundantly in marshy and alluvial soils, in slaughter-houses, common-sewers, dissecting-rooms, graveyards, and in those places where a large number of living persons are crowded to-gether, particularly if the effluvia of their excretions taint the atmosphere. Such places are called centres or foci of infection, because from the morbid influence there concentrated, disease spreads in every direction." [31] The infectious agents or miasms were usually supposed to enter the system through the lungs. Contagious diseases "strictly so called" were those "which can-not be traced to any other source than communication mediate or immediate with persons already attacked by them, and which cannot be referred to any atmospheric or other external cause, or combination of causes, but only to pre-existent causes of the same kind . . . ." [32]

The existing confusion can best be documented by another quotation from the same author, Stillé of Philadelphia.

A cargo of rags from the Levant arrives at one of our ports, and on being discharged, creates disease in all the neighbourhood of the vessel; if the disease thus originating is like one which was prevalent at the place whence the cargo came, the rags are a source of *contagion*. If there is no such similarity, or there was no prevalent disease at the Eastern port, then the newly-arisen malady must be attri-buted to the filth of the cargo, which is, in that case, a source of infection. [33]

No wonder that there was violent disagreement over the infec-tious or contagious character of such diseases as plague, cholera, and yellow fever! [34] This controversy was embittered by the

[31] Alfred Stillé, *Elements of General Pathology*, Philadelphia, 1848, p. 95.
[32] *Ibid.*, p. 100.   [33] *Ibid.*, p. 101.
[34] See Erwin H. Ackerknecht, Anticontagionism between 1821 and 1867, *Bull. Hist. Med.*, 1948, vol. 22, pp. 562-593.

practical consequences that if these diseases were contagious, ships from suspected countries had to be quarantined for a lengthy period of time. The confusion was further heightened by the assumption of "septic poisons, or those which are generated by putrefaction," and were believed to enter the body with the food, through the air, or "through a wound as so frequently happens to those engaged in anatomical studies." [35] But whether infection or contagion, the question remained how the virus acted in the body from the moment of its introduction to the outbreak of the disease. Stillé cites Liebig as believing in a fermentative action comparable to that of yeast. "Other observers," he adds, "upon the ground of an alleged discovery, that leaven acts by propagating vegetable germs, suppose the different sorts of virus to contain animal ova, or vegetable germs, which, by rapid generation, fill the body with parasitic insects or invisible plants, whose presence constitutes the disease." Stillé recommends waiting till the microscope has "revealed the existence of either of these sorts of bodies." [36]

We have cited Stillé's work at some length as a representative example of generally accepted medical theory. The book appeared in 1848 when the great sanitary movement was under way in England and when demands for public health reform were heard on the Continent as well. If it is true that the insight into the nature of infectious disease had not changed much between 1550 and 1850, then the intensification of the fight against infection must be due to other factors which had relatively little to do with an understanding of its mechanism.

---

[35] Stillé, *op. cit.*, p. 93.
[36] *Ibid.*, p. 104 f.

IV

Viewed in long-range perspective, the intensification of the fight against "filth" that animated the sanitarians can be seen as a stage in the process of civilization, a consequence of the ever increasing interdependence of men since the Middle Ages.[37] It can also be seen as specifically conditioned by industrialization, urbanization, and outbreaks of cholera,[38] and facilitated by the use of statistical methods. In addition, however, it can be understood as a changing attitude towards cleanliness.

Looking backwards we have difficulties in gauging the degree of cleanliness of past ages as judged by modern standards.[39] We are too easily misled by superficial analogies with our customs and their allegedly rational motives. For instance, the medieval custom of frequenting a bathhouse has been hailed as an important chapter in the history of hygiene. Undoubtedly persons bathing regularly will acquire a certain degree of cleanliness, although bathing is of little avail if the clothes are not kept clean too.[40] There are even medieval pictures showing groups of people using a tub and otherwise cleaning themselves. But other pictures, showing men and women bathing together, eating, drinking, and listening to music, indicate that the main attraction was not cleanliness but pleasure or the medicinal effect of water.[41]

[37] Norbert Elias, *Über den Prozess der Zivilisation*, 2 vols., Basel, Haus zum Falken, 1939.

[38] See above, p. 133.

[39] Material bearing on this and related questions will be found in Cabanès, *Mœurs intimes du passé*, Paris, Albert Michel; Norbert Elias, *op. cit.*, and Reginald Reynolds, *Cleanliness and Godliness*, New York, Doubleday and Company, 1946.

[40] This has been emphasized by J. F. D. Shrewsbury, The Plague of Athens, *Bull. Hist. Med.*, 1950, vol. 24, p. 11.

[41] The medicinal effect of bathing has to be clearly separated from its hygienic one. According to Meuli, Scythica, *Hermes*, 1935, vol. 70, pp. 121-

As late as 1752, a passage in Smollett's *Essay on the External Use of Water*, one of the few medical writings of the novelist, expresses the traditional evaluation. " Indeed," he writes, " the warm Bath is so well understood in its Anodyne capacity, that every body (almost) after the fatigue of a journey, or other hard exercise, has recourse to the Bagnio for refreshment: and so agreeable is the operation of this medicine, that in ancient times, as well as in these days, it has been considered as a point of *luxury* and *pleasure* . . . ." [42]

At the same time, the religious and ceremonial meaning of purity or cleanliness still stands very much in the foreground. Thus the large German encyclopedia published by Zedler around 1750 contains detailed discussions of the meaning of purity in the Bible, while the same entries have nothing to say about worldly cleanliness. A book by the famous Dr. Friedrich Hoff-mann, that appeared in 1722 and described how to enjoy health and long life in conformity with the teachings of Holy Writ, is a popular text on personal hygiene.[43] It mentions food, drink, the use of wine, baths, and tobacco—with hardly a word about cleanliness.

All this goes to show that as late as the eighteenth century the avoidance or removal of substances because of their poten-

---

176, there is also a relationship between the Finnish bath and shamanism. For pictorial material see Alfred Martin, *Deutsches Badewesen in vergangenen Tagen*, Jena, Diederichs, 1906.

[42] Tobias Smollett, *An Essay on the External Use of Water*, edited with introduction and notes by Claude E. Jones, Baltimore, The Johns Hopkins Press, 1935, p. 61 (italics mine). Praise and blame of bathing can be found in Martial's epigrams and is succinctly expressed in the *School of Salernum, loc. cit.*, p. 84:

> " *Wine, women, Baths, by Art or Nature warme,*
> *Us'd or abus'd do men much good or harme.*"

[43] Herrn Friederich Hoffmanns *Gruendlicher Unterricht* etc., Ulm, Daniel Bartholomäi, 1722.

tially harmful physiological action has not yet become the leading concept in the idea of cleanliness. This "physiological concept" of cleanliness is however gaining ground, especially, it would appear, in the Anglo-Saxon countries, concomitant with sanitary reforms in the army, navy, and jails.

It has been stated that cleanliness used to be a matter of aesthetics.[44] The truth of this is confirmed by Francis Bacon's dictum: "For cleanness, and the *civil beauty* of the Body was ever esteemed to proceed from a modesty of behaviour, and a due reverence *in the first place* towards God, whose creatures we are, then towards society, wherein we live; and then our selves, whom we ought no less, nay, much more to revere, than we do any others."[45] These lines occur under "Cosmetic" which, according to Bacon, relates to the beauty of the body rather than to its health. Shortly afterwards, the theme is taken up by George Herbert who demands of the country parson that "his apparrell [be] plaine, but reverend and clean, without spots, or dust, or smell; the purity of his mind breaking out and dilating it selfe even to his body, cloaths, and habitation."[46] Elsewhere Herbert generalizes this sentiment in the following verses:

> *Affect in things about thee cleanlinesse,*
> *That all may gladly board thee, as a flowre.*
> *Slovens take up their stock of noisomnesse*
> *Beforehand, and anticipate their last houre.*

---

[44] Henry E. Sigerist, *Civilization and Disease*, Cornell University Press, 1943, p. 26.

[45] Francis Bacon, *Of the Advancement and Proficiencie of Learning*, Interpreted by Gilbert Wats, London, 1674, Book 4, ch. 2, p. 130.

[46] The Country Parson, ch. 3, in: *The English Works of George Herbert*, ed. G. H. Palmer, 3 vols., Boston and New York, Houghton Mifflin and Company, 1905; vol. 1, p. 214. The parson is also to teach that "after religion . . . three things make a compleate servant: Truth, and Diligence, and Neatnesse or Cleanlinesse" (*ibid.*, p. 237).

> *Let thy minde's sweetnesse have his operation*
> *Upon thy body, clothes, and habitation.*[47]

The last two lines are used by John Wesley in 1791 in his sermon " On Dress," in which he argues that " slovenliness is no part of religion " and that Scripture nowhere " condemns neatness of apparel. Certainly this is a duty, not a sin. ' Cleanliness is, indeed, next to godliness.' Agreeably to this, good Mr. Herbert advises every one that fears God:—

> *Let thy mind's sweetness have its operation*
> *Upon thy person, clothes, and habitation.*

And surely every one should attend to this, if he would not have the good that is in him evil spoken of." [48]

It has been noticed long ago that Wesley refers to " Cleanliness is next to godliness " as to a proverb.[49] However that may be, the significance of the quotation does not lie in the expression of a new truth; rather it lies in the religious fervor with which " the lower and middle ranks of life," i. e., those whom scripture forbids " to be adorned with gold, or pearls, or costly apparel," [50] are admonished to keep themselves clean in appearance. Wesley wanted the dress of the Methodist to be plain as well as cheap. This meant that he could not easily hide dirt under perfumes and fashionable clothes. To the Methodist—as probably to the Quaker and others before him—cleanliness becomes a sign of respectability, and that means that even the respectable poor are now expected to avoid dirt.

Significantly enough, the stress on the religious meaning of

[47] The Church Porch, LXII, *ibid.*, vol. 2, p. 57.

[48] John Wesley, " Sermon 88, On Dress " in *Works*, vol. 7, fifth edition, London, 1860, p. 16. For the date, 1791, see *N. E. D. s. v.* " Cleanliness."

[49] W. Davenport Adams, *Dictionary of English Literature*, new and revised edition, London, Paris and New York, Cassell Potter and Galpin, p. 138.

[50] John Wesley, *loc. cit.*, p. 17.

cleanliness is paralleled by increasing emphasis upon its medical meaning. As a preacher, John Wesley quoted Herbert; as a lay medical adviser he quoted the physician George Cheyne. The latter, in his *Essay of Health and Long Life*, had said: " Every one, in order to preserve their Health, ought to observe all the Cleanness and Sweetness in their Houses, Cloaths, and Furniture, suitable to their Condition." [51] With slight changes, these lines reappear in the preface to John Wesley's *Primitive Physic*, dated 1747.[52]

There are other voices, apart from Wesley's, praising the medical and moral virtues of cleanliness. Dr. William Buchan, in his famous *Domestic Medicine*, a popular medical handbook, has a chapter " Of Cleanliness " in which it is recommended " as necessary for supporting the honour and dignity of human nature, as agreeable and useful to society, and as highly conducive to the preservation of health." [53] Reversing the order,

[51] George Cheyne, *An Essay of Health and Long Life,* London, 1724, p. 18. The particular meaning of these words evinces from p. 12: " Nor shall I add any pressing instances, to avoid *wet* Rooms, *damp* Beds, and *foul* Linnen, or to remove *Ordure* and *Nusances*; the Luxury of *England* having run all these rather into a *Vice*."

[52] John Wesley, *Primitive Physic:* or, An Essay and Natural Method of Curing most Diseases. Twenty-first edition, London, 1785, p. xiii: " Every one that would preserve health, should be as clean and sweet as possible in their houses, clothes and furniture." The date of the preface is given on p. xvi. The role of John Wesley in the spread of a " health " movement has probably been over-emphasized by Sir George Newman, *Health and Social Evolution,* London, Allen and Unwin, 1931, p. 61; cf. Shryock, *op. cit.*, p. 90. Moreover, Sir MacFarlane Burnet, in the *Lancet* of Jan. 17, 1953, p. 103, has drawn attention to the efforts made in the nineteenth century to impart the relatively high standards of cleanliness of upper class society to its lower strata. But it seems nevertheless important to note the currents among other than aristocratic and well-to-do circles.

[53] William Buchan, *Domestic Medicine:* or, A Treatise on the Prevention and Cure of Diseases by Regimen and Simple Medicines. Second edition, London, 1772, p. 131. The whole chapter (VIII) is worth attention because of the inferences it allows to the widespread prejudice against cleanliness in the case of sick people.

John Pringle, the British army physician, says: "Cleanliness is conducive to health, but is it not obvious, that it also tends to good order and other virtues?"[54] And Benjamin Rush, who quotes these lines with approval, states that "too much cannot be said in favour of cleanliness, as a physical means of promoting virtue."[55]

The insistence on cleanliness is vague as long as it is not accompanied by definite requirements. In 1794, Dr. Hufeland, in his treatise on long life, suggested not only daily washing but even, if possible, a daily change of linen.[56] For the majority of the population, the latter was as yet a utopian demand. However, the introduction of the Leblanc process, in 1791, for the manufacture of soda, and the contemporary revolution in the cotton industry laid the preconditions for an eventual realization of this utopia. At any event, by the end of the eighteenth century, the physiological concept of cleanliness had not only been greatly advanced over previous times but had also become imbued with a moral and religious force. Cleanliness was trans-

[54] Quoted from Benjamin Rush, *An Inquiry into the Influence of Physical Causes upon the Moral Faculty* (1786), Philadelphia, 1839, p. 15. Rush refers to Pringle's "oration upon Captain Cook's Voyage, delivered before the Royal Society in London" as his source (*ibid.*). In his *Observations on the Diseases of the Army,* seventh edition, London, 1775, p. 92. Pringle writes that "officers judge rightly with respect to the health of the men, as well as to their appearance, when they require cleanness both in their persons and clothes." Remarkably enough, he believes that "plague, pestilential fevers, putrid scurvies, and dysenteries, have abated in Europe within this last century; a blessing which we can attribute to no other second cause, than to our improvement in every thing relating to cleanliness, and to the more general use of antiseptics" (p. 332). Regarding London, he admits that there is room for hygienic improvement, but adds that "some of the main points have been well attended to; such as regard the privies, the common sewers, and the supplies of fresh water; and the people in general are very cleanly" (p. 335).

[55] Rush, *loc. cit.*

[56] Christopher William Hufeland, *The Art of Prolonging Life.* Translated from the German, 2 vols., London, 1797; see vol. 2, p. 236.

ferred from the domain of cosmetics to that of health, and with
the Enlightenment, the appeal to health became an ever more
powerful motive for action. Guided by their own rationalization
of life, men also rationalized the past. The laws of the Bible
imposing the ritualistic stamp of clean and unclean were now
explained as wise sanitary prescriptions by a shrewd law giver.[57]
This change in the mentality of modern man also brought about
a change in his concept of infection.

V

The nineteenth century completed what we may call the secularization of the concept of infection by redirecting the basic
meaning of the term, by giving it a new scientific content and
a new moral force. If we look up the words "infection" and
"to infect" in the New English Dictionary, we find that the
medical meaning is emerging as the most concrete one. The
notion of immersing or staining an object has become obsolete
and so has the notion of impurity in the chemical sense of an
alloy or the adulteration of a substance. The medical meaning,
in various shades, stands in the foreground and overshadows the
other broader meanings of corruption and defilement. The latter
still exist but seem relegated to the status of similes and metaphors. Such a semantic circle was made possible by the purge
to which the Enlightenment of the eighteenth century had
subjected everything "superstitious." But the semantic change
could not have been achieved without filling the notion of
infection with a more strictly scientific content than it had had
before. This was done by the rising science of bacteriology
which substituted pathogenic microorganisms for the miasmata,
contagia, effluvia, and corruptions of old. It would be repetitious

---

[57] See e. g. Rush, *loc. cit.*

to recount the well-known tales of Schwann who proved that putrefaction needed an external agent; of his colleague Henle, at the Berlin laboratory of Müller, who postulated the identity of contagions and miasms, believing in the organic nature of both; of Josiah Nott's animalcular theory of the transmission of yellow fever; and of John Snow's theory of cholera propounded a few years later. The endeavors of these and many others prepared the way for Pasteur's investigations and the work of Robert Koch and Joseph Lister. Much resistance had to be overcome, yet by 1900 the victory was complete. To dwell upon the progress which has since been made would be to repeat another often told tale. Instead we had better sum up what we have said so far.

We started out with the observation that our modern medical concept of infection emerged from the notion of ritualistic or religious pollution of which disease was but one type. The Greek physicians accepted this older terminology, at the same time giving it a naturalistic turn. This was the first secularization of the concept. I must leave it to those better trained psychologically to decide how successful this turn was. I expect that they will claim that a good deal of the dread of higher powers and of feelings of guilt still are hidden in our minds. During the Middle Ages and Renaissance we found a progressive recognition of what, today, we call infectious diseases. The belief in disease entities of a specific character was strengthened in the nineteenth century by the discovery of bacteria as specific etiologic agents. The interpretation of infection as resulting from filth guided public health measures in the medieval cities as well as in the industrial centers of the early nineteenth century. The notion proved insufficient and was replaced by deepened scientific insight. But the emergence of nineteenth century hygiene and bacteriology and asepsis were themselves conditioned upon willingness to rationalize the conduct of life in accordance with medical rules. This process, initiated in the eighteenth century by a widening regard for individual cleanliness, led to the second secularization of the concept of infection. The medical meaning of the word, backed throughout by the sciences of bacteriology and immunology, has become the prime meaning.

These are the structural elements of the concept of infection which our historical analysis has revealed to us. To check its completeness we turn once more to the definition from which we started. Infection, we read, is an " invasion of the tissues of the body by pathogenic organisms . . . ." We may stop here and wonder again about the use of the curious word " invasion," reminiscent of hostile armies whose onslaught ought to be resisted. If we had looked up another dictionary we might have found another word instead of " invasion." Yet some image seems necessary to explain the encounter between the human being and his enemies, the pathogenic organisms.

In its early enthusiasm of some seventy years ago, the bacteriological school believed that man plus germ equalled disease. It was then realized that the matter was not so simple and that natural or acquired immunity and somatic as well as psychic disposition had to be taken into account in order to explain why some people fall ill, while others remain healthy; and why the same person may long harbor germs before the germs suddenly produce disease. It was during that period that Dr. Ottmar Rosenbach, in an essay still worth reading, pointed out the similarity between the old protective measures against evil spirits defiling man's soul and the extreme bacteriologist's endeavor to protect the welfare of the body.[58] Far from accepting Dr. Rosenbach's analysis as criticism, I believe that he really laid bare a necessary desideratum. As long as infection was held

[58] O. Rosenbach, *Physician versus Bacteriologist*, New York and London, 1904, p. 247.

to be a pollution, it was understandable in human terms. It was punishment for a trespass, a sin, or a crime, or merely the danger threatening from a supernatural power. At any rate, man thought he knew why he had become infected.

The nineteenth century tried to break radically with this anthropomorphic heritage. It succeeded as far as the explanation of the mechanism of infection is concerned. The bacteriologist's job was to find out what happened after man and germ had met. Why had they met? As far as the bacteriologist was concerned, this question was irrelevant. " By accident," he might say, if an answer was insisted upon. But as a physician, or public health officer, or citizen, the same bacteriologist took quite a different attitude. The more he came to know about the mechanics of infection, the more he believed that he knew how infection could and should be avoided. Responsibility for the prevention and cure of infection has now become a moral and even political force which it never was before. This being the case, our attitude has to be acknowledged as part of our concept of infection. In defining infection as an injury caused by an invasion by pathogenic microorganisms, we indicate our readiness to resist them. Modern physics boastfully or plaintively speaks of the meaningless universe. But there is no meaningless universe in medicine. Human beings are not satisfied with viewing health and disease as matters of mere chance separable from their lives. Health, diseases, recovery, and other medical categories mark biological conditions as desirable or undesirable. The latter characteristic accounts for the medical nature of the concept of infection and for its persistence under different cultural conditions with different notions about the fight against pollution.

BENTLEY GLASS

The Long Neglect of a Scientific Discovery: Mendel's Laws of Inheritance

⋙⋙⋙⋙⋙⋙⋙⋙⋙⋙⋙⋙

The extraordinary neglect of Mendel's work from the time of its presentation in 1865 and its publication in 1866 until its rediscovery in 1900 constitutes a major riddle in the history of scientific ideas. Many suggestions have been made to account for this failure on the part of Mendel's contemporaries to see the import of his discoveries, and it is the purpose of this brief chapter to re-examine the question and to reappraise the various theories which have been offered.

One may dispose most readily of the frequently made suggestion that Mendel's work was ignored because it was presented to an obscure natural history society and published in its equally obscure proceedings. It is, of course, true that the *Naturforschender Verein* in Brünn was not one of the most notable scientific academies of Europe; but it was by no means unrecognized, and its proceedings were exchanged, according to Bateson, "with most of the Academies of Europe, including both the Royal and Linnean Societies." [1] The *Verhandlungen* were sufficiently well-known for Mendel's two papers to be cited by Hoffmann in 1869 in a paper entitled "*Untersuchungen zur*

[1] W. Bateson. *Mendel's Principles of Heredity*, p. 316. Cambridge: at the University Press. xvi + 396 pp. 1909.

Bestimmung des Werthes von Species und Varietät: ein Beitrag zur Kritik der Darwin'schen Hypothese," [2] and again by Focke in 1881 in his *Pflanzenmischlinge*.[3] Focke's work was the standard reference on the subject for many years following its publication; and it is of interest that all three of the rediscoverers and verifiers of Mendel's work—Correns, von Tschermak, and de Vries—found their way to it either directly or indirectly through Focke's *Pflanzenmischlinge*.

Both Correns and von Tschermak were directed to the original by Focke's book, although Correns thereupon recalled having heard of it earlier from his teacher Nägeli.[4] Hugo de Vries found his way to Mendel by means of a reference in the American work, *Cross-Breeding and Hybridizing*, by L. H. Bailey (1891); [5] and Bailey [6] has recorded the fact that he had taken the reference, without seeing the original work by Mendel, from Focke's *Pflanzenmischlinge*. In fact, Bailey had sent to de Vries in 1892 a reprint of his lecture on "Crossbreeding and Hybridizing," which contained the reference to Mendel. Focke was himself asked by Iltis, the biographer of Mendel, how he had happened to become acquainted with Mendel's work, and Focke said, "I had become aware of Mendel's work through the literature of the 70's; however, I cannot say where I found it mentioned." [7] It therefore appears very likely that Focke himself

---

[2] Hermann Hoffmann. *Untersuchungen zur Bestimmung des Werthes von Species und Varietät: ein Beitrag zur Kritik der Darwin'schen Hypothese.* Giessen, 1869. 179 pp.

[3] Wilhelm Olbers Focke. *Die Pflanzenmischlinge, ein Beitrag zur Biologie der Gewächse.* Berlin, 1881. 596 pp.

[4] H. F. Roberts. *Plant Hybridization before Mendel,* p. 338. Princeton University Press, Princeton, 1929. xvi + 374 pp.

[5] L. H. Bailey. *Cross-Breeding and Hybridizing.* Rural Pub. Co., New York. 1891. [Included in *Plant Breeding,* 1895.]

[6] Roberts, ibid., p. 323.

[7] Hugo Iltis. *Gregor Johann Mendel: Leben, Werk und Werkung,*

found the reference in the work of Hoffmann. This Hoffmann is the same botanist whose works were well known to Darwin, who discussed Hoffmann's crosses with radishes in *Animals and Plants under Domestication* (1868) [8] and his extensive selection experiment with the bean *Phaseolus* in *The Effects of Cross- and Self-fertilization* (1876) .[9] The latter experiments were reported in the very brochure mentioned above as containing the reference to Mendel's work, and this brochure was actually cited by Darwin as his own source. It is therefore possible, as Punnett pointed out in 1925, that Darwin had the reference to Mendel's work before him some four or five years after its publication.[10]

One of the most remarkable reasons given for the neglect of Mendel is that which is attributed to J. B. S. Haldane by Wightman.[11] According to the latter, Haldane has suggested that the reason may have been the lack of stimulus to plant-breeding in Britain as a result of the repeal of the Corn Laws. This gratuitous effort to force the social interpretation of science into the question scarcely deserves refutation. In the first place, it limits the neglect of Mendel to Britain when it was actually world-wide. In the second place, even in Britain it was clearly not the case. No one was more interested in plant hybridization than Darwin, and his influence alone was enough to lend great

J. Springer, Berlin. 1924. [Eng. trans., Allen & Unwin, London; W. W. Norton, New York. 1932.] "Auf Mendels Arbeit bin ich durch die Literatur der 70er Jahre aufmerksam geworden, kann aber nicht sagen, wo ich sie erwähnt gefunden habe."

[8] Charles Darwin. *The Variation of Animals and Plants under Domestication,* Second Edition, Vol. I, p. 345. Appleton & Co., New York. 1897. [First Edition, 1868.]

[9] Charles Darwin. *The Effects of Cross- and Self-Fertilisation in the Vegetable Kingdom,* p. 151. Appleton, New York. 1877.

[10] R. C. Punnett. An early reference to Mendel's work. *Nature, Lond.,* 116: 606. 1925.

[11] William P. D. Wightman. *The Growth of Scientific Ideas,* p. 460. Yale University Press, New Haven. xii + 495 pp. 1951.

importance to any subject. A similar view, suggested by Wightman, is that perhaps the "ruling liberal dogma of progress prejudiced minds otherwise alert and critical in favour of the possibility of unlimited selection." [12] It might be more correct to go straight to the chief support of the dogma of progress, the social interpretation of the theory of organic evolution, as the reason. Yet here again it would seem unwise to impute such blindness to the open-minded, thorough, critical Darwin himself, no matter how many Darwinians might be purblind. Anyway, it would scarcely have occurred to plant-breeders in the 1860's and 1870's that the Mendelian principles were an obstacle to the theory of selection. Mendel himself, according to his biographer Iltis, accepted evolution "and was suspected as a Darwinist not without reason." To Mendel the laws he had discovered were a disclosure of the mechanism of evolution through the combination and recombination of hereditary elements. Mendel also accepted the theory of natural selection, to judge from a passage in his last letter to Nägeli:

> If that were the situation we would have to attribute the spontaneous hybridization in Hieracium to temporary disturbances which, if often repeated and becoming permanent, would finally result in the disappearance of that particular species; whereas one or another of the more favorably organized hybrids, which might be better adapted to the existing conditions, might succeed in maintaining itself in the struggle for existence, and in continuing for long periods of time until ultimately it, too, would suffer the same fate.[13]

There is no trace of feeling here of any incompatibility between

[12] *Ibid.*, p. 460.

[13] Hugo Iltis. "Gregor Mendel's Life and Heritage," pp. 30-32, in *Genetics in the 20th Century* (L. C. Dunn, ed.), pp. 25-34. Macmillan, New York. 1951.

Mendelian heredity and natural selection. Nor is it to be believed that it prevailed in Britain any more than in the mind of Mendel himself. Bateson, the outstanding student of plant and animal variation as the basis of evolution, became an immediate protagonist of Mendelism in 1900, and built the science of genetics in that country against the opposition of Galtonian ideas of heredity and of the biometricians, represented by Karl Pearson. At the same time, in the Netherlands, the Mendelist Hugo de Vries made genetic change the basis of his evolutionary masterwork, *The Mutation Theory*.

The fact is, as Conway Zirkle has pointed out, that Darwin in 1868 actually found in his own plant-breeding a clear-cut case of Mendelian inheritance, which he failed to analyze sufficiently.[14] Having crossed snapdragons and produced hybrid varieties, Darwin found what he called " prepotency "—and what Mendel called " dominance "—in the first generation offspring. What is more, he obtained both parental types in the second generation of hybrids, actually counted the number of each kind, and found 88 of the prepotent type, 37 of the other. This result is not significantly different from a Mendelian 3 : 1 ratio, but Darwin did not know how to attribute meaning to it. Surely, if Darwin had actually had the chance to see Mendel's superbly clear account, he would have recognized its validity. Mendel's own modesty, which prevented him from sending any copy of his papers to the great evolutionist, was largely responsible. In his later years, when he stubbornly but bitterly said, as he often did, " *Meine Zeit wird schon kommen*," [15] the thought that he

[14] Conway Zirkle. " The Knowledge of Heredity before 1900," p. 50, in *Genetics in the 20th Century*, pp. 35-57. 1951.

Charles Darwin. *The Variation of Animals and Plants Under Domestication*, 2nd ed.; Vol. II, p. 46. 1897. [1868].

[15] Bateson, *ibid.*, p. 314.

himself might have altered it all seems not to have crossed his mind.

Far more plausible than the views already considered is the probability that the minds of the plant-breeders and hybridizers, British, German, and French alike, were so obsessed by the overwhelming interest in the origin of species that they were concerned only with the crosses and hybrids *between* species. This had been from the time of Linnaeus and Kölreuter the object of great researches. We find Darwin, in a letter to Hooker, deploring the fact that no one had translated Gärtner's works into English and made them generally accessible to English-speaking scientists.[16] Nägeli completely ignores the crosses Mendel has made between varieties of peas, and pays attention only to his crosses of species of *Hieracium*. Focke, too, was much more concerned with the species crossed, as one can tell from the frequency of his mention of Mendel's work (15 references) in comparison with his references to the work by Gärtner (409), Kölreuter (214), Herbert (155), Godron (102), Naudin (89), or others who hybridized species. It was all a part of the greatly intensified interest in evolution, and, as Roberts says, " It was supposedly not at all conceivable, that the laws of hybrid breeding could be compassed within a series of experiments upon a single plant." [17]

That Darwin could have ignored so obvious a lead as Hoffmann's reference to Mendel, when one considers Darwin's enormous interest in this field and the intensity with which he pursued the work of the hybridizers in other countries, is indeed surprising. Had he considered, from Hoffmann's reference, that Mendel's work contained anything of value, he would surely

[16] Francis Darwin (ed.). *More Letters of Charles Darwin*, Vol. II, p. 340. Appleton, New York. 1903.

[17] Roberts, *ibid.*, p. 211.

have written Mendel for a copy of the paper, though he might have obtained it even in England. Hoffmann's comments thus become most interesting. He referred to "Mendel's six-year-long observations," but seems to have regarded the main point as the finding that *Pisum* is self-fertilized. He summarized Mendel's results as follows: "Hybrids possess the tendency in the succeeding generations to revert to the parent species." [18] This would certainly not have been sufficient to stimulate Darwin's curiosity to know more about Mendel's experiments, for Darwin was well acquainted with the work of Kölreuter, Gärtner, Herbert, Knight, Nägeli, Godron, Naudin, Lecoq, Wichura, and other plant hybridizers, all of whom had described in much more precise terms than this reference their own results of a similar nature. What is even more surprising is the lack of any reference by Hoffmann to the experiments done by Mendel on *Phaseolus* and reported in the same paper as confirming the mode of inheritance found for the characters studied in *Pisum*. Either Hoffmann did not read Mendel's paper through to the end, or he discounted its value completely.

Although Focke referred to Mendel's work no less than fifteen times in his book, it was again with little understanding. The most important reference, under the heading of *Pisum*, is as follows: "Mendel's numerous crosses yielded results that were entirely similar to those of Knight, yet Mendel believed he found constant numerical proportions between the types of hybrids. In general the seeds produced by a hybrid pollination retain, also in peas, exactly the form and color which characterizes the mother-plant, even when from these very seeds plants arise that completely resemble the male parent, and which

[18] Hoffmann, *ibid.*, p. 136. "Hybride besitzen die Neigung, in den folgenden Generationen in die Stammarten zurückzuschlagen."

thereupon also bring forth seeds of the same sort." [19] He promises to carry the discussion further under the section on Xenia (which we would now term "dominance"), but by the time he has reached that section he has forgotten, and Mendel is not rementioned. Focke was a reasonably critical synthesizer of his chosen field, but how can one explain so gross a misinterpretation as the above of Mendel's clearly worded statement: " It was further proved by all of the experiments that it is completely immaterial whether the dominating character comes from the seed- or the pollen-parent; the form of the hybrid remains in both cases exactly the same." [20]

The result of this consideration is to indicate that failure to comprehend, and not inaccessibility of the work, was the reason for the neglect of Mendel's discovery. Yet the failure of Hoffmann and later of Focke to understand Mendel's work pales into insignificance beside the lack of comprehension on the part of Nägeli. Where Hoffmann was interested chiefly in selection rather than crossing, and Focke was a compiler of true German thoroughness who did very little experimental hybridization himself, Nägeli was a plant hybridizer of great renown and was particularly interested in the genus *Hieracium,* to which Mendel

---

[19] Focke, *ibid.*, p. 110. " Mendels zahlreiche Kreuzungen ergaben Resultate, die den Knight'schen ganz ähnlich waren, doch glaubte Mendel constante Zahlenverhältnisse zwischen den Typen der Mischlinge zu finden. Im Allgemeinen behalten die durch eine hybride Bestäubung erzeugten Samen auch bei den Erbsen genau die Gestalt und Farbe bei, welche der Mutterpflanze zukommt, auch wenn aus diesen Samen selbst Pflanzen hervorgehen, welche ganz der Vaterpflanze gleichen und welche dann auch deren Samen bringen."

[20] Gregor Johann Mendel. Versuche über Pflanzen-Hybriden. *Verh. naturf. Ver. Brünn,* Abhandlungen, 4: 3-47. 1866. [Facsimile reprint in *J. Hered.,* 42: 3-47.] " Es wurde ferner durch sämmtliche Versuche erwiesen, dass es völlig gleichgiltig ist, ob das dominirende Merkmal der Samen- oder Pollenpflanze angehört; die Hybridform bleibt in beiden Fällen genau dieselbe." (p. 11).

devoted his second paper, that of 1869.[21] Beginning in 1866, Mendel wrote Nägeli no less than ten letters, with the first of which he enclosed a copy of the famous paper on *Pisum* and *Phaseolus*.[22] In the second letter he carefully and painstakingly re-explained his results in considerable detail, and added much information about his hybridizations between species in the genera *Hieracium, Geum, Aquilegia, Cirsium, Linaria*, and others. At Nägeli's own request, he sent him some seeds of *Pisum* from the small remaining store left after devastations of the pea beetle. In return, Nägeli sent reprints and later some seeds of *Hieracium*, the receipt of which was gratefully acknowledged by Mendel.

In 1869, Mendel sent Nägeli thirty-one hybrid plants from his own *Hieracium* crosses; and a reciprocal exchange of plants continued until the termination of the correspondence in 1873. In 1870, Mendel reported to Nägeli the conclusion of experiments with *Matthiola annua* and *M. glabra*, with *Zea,* and with *Mirabilis*, all of whose hybrids behave exactly like those of *Pisum*. Later in the same year he reported a 3 female : 1 male ratio for sex in a cross between *Lychnis diurna* and *L. vespertina*. Notwithstanding this close and apparently friendly relationship, Nägeli never so much as mentioned Mendel's work, even that with *Hieracium,* in any of numerous contributions on the subject nor in his ultimate masterwork, the *Mechanisch-physiologische Theorie der Abstammungslehre* (1884), published in the year before Mendel died.[23] It was not that Nägeli had forgotten the

[21] Gregor Johann Mendel. Über einige aus künstlicher Befruchtung gewonnene Hieracium-Bastarde. *Verh. naturf. Ver. Brünn,* Abhandlungen, 8: 26-32. 1870. [Translated in Bateson, *ibid.,* 362-368.]

[22] Gregor Mendel's Letters to Carl Nägeli, 1866-1873, published by Carl Correns, *Abh. math.-phys. Kl. kgl. sächs. Gesell. Wiss.,* 29: 189-265. 1905. [Translated, *Genetics,* 35 (5, Part 2): 1-29. 1950.]

[23] Carl von Nägeli. *Mechanisch-physiologische Theorie der Abstammungslehre.* R. Oldenbourg, München and Leipzig. xii + 822 pp. 1884.

Augustinian abbot. Carl Correns has stated that, in addition to his own knowledge of the monograph by Focke, he knew of Mendel also through his teacher Nägeli: " Besides through Focke's book, I had been made cognizant of Mendel's investigations through my teacher Nägeli. And I believe also to remember that he told me of Mendel, but certainly only of the *Hieracium* investigations, in which alone he was permanently interested. . . ." [24]

It seems evident, then, that Nägeli completely failed to appreciate the significance of Mendel's discoveries. For this there seems to have been a variety of reasons. Nägeli was above all an idealist. His conversion from a career in medicine to one in botany came about through the effect produced upon him by the " ideal urge " [*ideales Streben*] of his teacher Oken, that most mystical of all the *Naturphilosophes*.[25] Although he later studied Hegelian philosophy for two years, Nägeli sharply defended himself against any imputation that he was himself a Hegelian. His cleavage with Darwin over the Theory of Natural Selection he attributed to the weakness of Darwin's theory in supplying specific physical and chemical causes for evolutionary change. His own " mechanical-physiological theory " likened the micellae of living substance to the crystals of the inorganic world. Thus from a conceptual structure he derived a vast Theory of Direct Evolutionary Action. "According to the theory of the direct action, on the contrary, the structure and function of the organism in its principal characteristics is a necessary consequence of forces dwelling within the substance and thereby independent of external chances." [26] This " perfecting force " [*Vervollkomm-*

[24] Roberts, *ibid.*, p. 338. Letter from Carl Correns, Jan. 30, 1925.

[25] E. Rádl. *Geschichte der biologischen Theorien seit dem Ende des siebzehnten Jahrhunderts*. W. Engelmann, Leipzig. 1905-1909. [Eng. trans., Oxford University Press, 1930.]

[26] Nägeli, *ibid.*, p. 294. " Nach der Theorie der directen Bewirkung dagegen ist Bau und Function der Organismen in Hauptzügen eine nothwendige Folge

nungskraft], as he termed it, is the evolutionary counterpart of Goethe's and Haeckel's " inner formative force " [*innere Bildungstrieb*], and leaves to Natural Selection only the accessory job of trimming away the imperfect branches of the tree of life. (Note the similarity to Bergson's *élan vital.*)

The consequence, it seems, of Nägeli's thinking in such a mode, of fitting the organism into his conceptual pattern, was to lead him to despise the work of Mendel as purely limited and empirical. This tendency appears to have carried over into the thinking of Weismann, Nägeli's most eminent pupil. Weismann's magnificent development on a conceptual basis of his theory of the ids (today read genes) —those hypothetical hereditary particles housed in the chromosomes and transmitted from generation to generation through the isolated, continuous germplasm—somehow failed to make him an immediate enthusiastic protagonist of Mendelism in 1900. In spite of the triple confirmation of Mendel's work, and in spite of the almost immediate and independent realization by Theodor Boveri in Germany and by W. S. Sutton in the United States that Mendelian behavior exactly parallels the behavior of the chromosomes in sexual reproduction, we find Weismann writing in 1902 with considerable reserve: " This led to the discovery that similar experiments had been published as far back as 1866 by the Abbot of Brünn, Gregor Mendel, and that these had been formulated as a law which is now called Mendel's law. Correns showed, however, that this law, though correct in certain cases, did not by any means hold good in all, and we must thus postpone the working of this new material into our theory until a very much wider basis of facts has been supplied by the botanists. There is less to be hoped for from the zoologists in regard to this problem

von der Substanz innewohnenden Kräften und somit unabhängig von äusseren Zufälligkeiten."

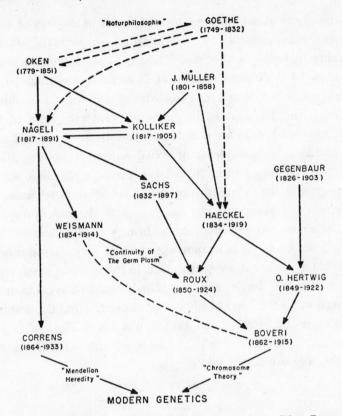

MODERN GENETICS

FIG. 1. THE CHAIN OF IDEAS FROM GOETHE AND OKEN, WHO REPRESENT THE NATURPHILOSOPHIE, TO MODERN GENETICS.

In addition to those persons mentioned in the text there are included, to show further influences, *Johannes Peter Müller*, who began with Naturphilosophie and ended in exact research in physiology, comparative anatomy, and marine biology; the great teacher *Rudolf Albert Kölliker*, a close friend of Nägeli, and one who taught not only Haeckel but Virchow and many other notable biologists, and who opposed Darwinism because he thought it teleological; *Carl Gegenbaur*, doctrinaire comparative anatomist and embryologist, whose foremost student, *Oskar Hertwig*, discoverer with others of mitotic cell-division and of fertilization, was also one of the most independent of Gegenbaur's disciples; *Julius Sachs*, student of Nägeli, and the founder of modern plant physiology, who held views of heredity like Weismann's; *Wilhelm Roux*, father of experimental embryology, co-discoverer with Hertwig of the union in fertilization of the nuclei of spermatozoon and egg-cell, and also with Hertwig, with whom he was on very bad terms, first to regard the chromosomes as the physical carriers of heredity; finally, *Theodor Boveri*, who did much to prove the persistent individuality of the chromosomes and to formulate and establish the Chromosome Theory of Heredity.

Gregor Mendel might be regarded as lying out to the side of all these streams of thought, and connecting with them only through *Carl Correns*.

owing to the almost insuperable difficulties in the way of a long series of experiments in hybridization in animals." [27] How lacking in foresight this was, Thomas Hunt Morgan was soon to show by the commencement of *Drosophila* breeding. Not all Weismann's insight and his knowledge of the similarity of mitosis, meiosis, and fertilization in plants and animals, from high to low, enabled him to see that Mendel's discovery was valid as far and wide as the prevalence of sexual reproduction. Fig. 1 illustrates the chain of ideas from Oken through Nägeli to various biologists of the twentieth century. Like all such schemes, it is selective and gives only the barest idea of the real multiplicity of influences. Nevertheless, in the history of ideas, the influence of teacher on pupil is in most instances of major significance.

What magnificent irony, therefore, in the fact that it was chiefly the conceptual developments of Nägeli's student Weismann that proved to be the necessary basis for understanding the empirical discoveries of Mendel, and that it was the student of Nägeli's old age, Carl Correns, who rediscovered and verified the work of the Augustinian prelate.

[27] August Weismann. *Vorträge über Deszendenztheorie*, 2nd ed., Vol. II, p. 49. 1904. [First Edition, 1902; Eng. trans., 1904.] " Man hat dabei die Entdeckung gemacht, dass ähnliche Versuche schon 1866 veröffentlicht worden waren, und zwar von dem Brünner Abt Gregor Mendel, der damals schon zu einem Gesetz oder einer Regel gekommen war, die man nun nach ihm die Mendelschen Regel nennt. Correns zeigt indessen, dass diese Regel, obgleich in gewissen Fällen richtig, doch keineswegs in allen gilt, und so werden wir die Einarbeitung dieses neuen Materials in unsere Theorie solange verschieben müssen, bis eine noch bedeutend breitere Basis von Tatsachen durch die Botaniker geschaffen sein wird. Von den Zoologen ist in dieser Frage weniger zu hoffen wegen der fast unüberwindlichen Schwierigkeiten, welche sich einer längeren Reihe von Kreuzungsversuchen bei Tieren entgegenstellen." (It is apparent that the translators have diminished the emphasis of these words.)

PHILIP P. WIENER

Lovejoy's Rôle in American Philosophy

➤➤➤➤➤➤➤➤➤➤➤➤➤➤➤➤➤➤➤

What a wonderfully discriminating and devastating essay Lovejoy could write on the plethora of diverse and incongruous
meanings of the abused terms "American" and "philosophy"!

Consider the diversity of ideas about Americans in: Buffon's
and Hegel's curious notions about the inferior size of moun-
tains, living things, and persons in America; James Fenimore
Cooper's stories of our Indians, whose war-paint and feathers
still stick to the European image of the American temperament;
the fiery sermons of Jonathan Edwards who converted Indians
and other Americans; Alexis de Tocqueville's and Charles
Dickens' views of Americans; Emerson's plea for the indepen-
dence of the American scholar; Henry James's American; the
gringo Yanqui despised by Latin-Americans; the Communist
Party's "twentieth-century Americanism" up to 1945 and anti-
American hate campaign after 1945; the K. K. K., Christian
Front, and McCarthyist notions of Americanism; the D. A. R.,
the A. D. A., the New, Fair, Square, and No Deal-ers' programs
to save America; Sinclair Lewis's optimistic and Theodore
Dreiser's tragic American; American tourists, expatriates, and
Fulbright Fellows abroad; the Anglo-, Dutch-, French-, Irish-,
Italian-, Jewish-, Oriental-, Polish-, Russian-, Scandinavian-,
Spanish-, and any other hyphenated Americans, recalling that
there is no other kind. One does not have to be a discriminating

Lovejoy to wonder what the specialists in "American Studies" mean by "the American mind."

Of course, this assortment of ideas about what an American is, does not imply that there is no such animal, any more than the historical fact that the American Constitution has been interpreted so differently by the courts at various times, and by experts in constitutional law at the sáme time, implies that we have no Constitution. Similarly, we have American philosophy, or better, philosophy in America; but do we have in fact or in desire *an* American Philosophy? Does the history of philosophy in the United States give us an unequivocal answer?

In colonial and theocratic New England, whom shall we declare to be the representatives of early American philosophy—the intolerant witch-hunter Cotton Mather or the more enlightened John Woolman, the tory Governor John Winthrop or the more liberal Roger Williams, Calvinistic original sin-ners like Edwards or Deistic free-thinkers like Paine? And when we move on to more recent times, would any be so foolhardy as to claim that American religious philosophy is represented fully by one or another of the sects of Congregationalists, Episcopalians (High or Low), Baptists, Methodists, Catholics, Jews (Orthodox or Reform), Christian Scientists, or Jehovah's Witnesses? In the history of our political philosophies who is more truly American—Thomas Jefferson or Alexander Hamilton, Andrew Jackson or John Adams and his line, Abe Lincoln or Stephen Douglas, General Grant or General Lee, Teddy or Franklin D. Roosevelt, Truman or Dewey, Adlai or Ike, Senator Morse or Senator McCarthy?

It may be objected that I have chosen the very controversial domains of religious and political philosophy, where unanimity is rare and difficult to establish. Then let us turn to the more objective field of the growth of the sciences in America. Here

162

we find two divergent views: the popular, that **Benjamin Franklin** and **Thomas Edison** represent the best tradition of Yankee
experimental inventiveness and practicality; and the scholarly,
that the less well-known scientific theorists like Josiah Willard
Gibbs, Joseph Henry, and Charles Peirce, more admirably represent the best in American science. Obviously, however, " American science " is as absurd a term as, e. g., " Russian science," so
far as anything inherent in the content or logic of science is concerned. And to the extent that an American philosopher is
scientific, he cannot in truth be propounding an " American "
philosophy.

When we come to "American Philosophy," the problem of
characterizing its distinctive features is complicated by the traditional lack of agreement among philosophers concerning the
nature of their discipline and its problems. Lovejoy has more
than once indicated that there is little hope for progress in
philosophy, in America or anywhere else, so long as there is so
little agreement about the method of resolving differences of
opinion on philosophical questions—in contrast with what we
find in the cumulative and cooperative growth of the sciences.
Lovejoy, we know, rejects methodolatry, the worship of method
apart from subject matter. He has not taken to the habit of
certain positivists of emasculating philosophy by elaborating
formal rules and criteria of meaning *überhaupt*. A keen student of natural languages and a masterful semasiologist, Lovejoy
could not accept the logical syntax or semantics of formalized
languages as providing *the* method of philosophy, although this
method of purging philosophy of its past disorders has been very
fashionable among younger American philosophers influenced by
Russell, Wittgenstein, and Carnap. Although *l'esprit de finesse*
is stronger in Lovejoy than *l'esprit géométrique*, I do not think
he would deny the value of symbolic logic for the analysis of

mathematical ideas. I believe he would say of such mathematical philosophizing what Aristotle said of the Pythagoreans, that number and spatial magnitude do not exhaust the categories of reality. The rapid advance of pure and applied mathematics in technological America has helped promote the vogue of logical or scientific empiricism among the younger philosophers here who wish to get away from the apparently futile verbal wrangling among the older American idealists, realists, and pragmatists of all stripes. Lovejoy, critical realist, also showed his discontent with the state of philosophy in America about fifty years ago by applying his critical and historical abilities to the analysis of the ambiguities of pragmatism, to an incisive attack on blanket monisms of all schools, and to the revitalization of the study of the history of philosophic ideas. Thus Lovejoy has done his superb share in making of philosophy in America not a logomachy, but a sustained search for the strands and patterns of ideas in the historical strife of philosophical systems, in literary works, arts and political movements, whenever they embody the products of scientific, aesthetic, and moral reflection—a search far closer to the actual modes of men's thinking than formal logic. If philosophy is to have a future in America, it will not only have to study the logic of the exact sciences, but will also, as Lovejoy has shown by his exemplary studies in the history of ideas, have to devote itself to methodological and philosophic clarification of ideas in the humanistic disciplines and social studies.

The problem of what constitutes the " American " components of " American philosophy " is a humanistic and social problem, and Lovejoy's method of resolving complexes of ideas into their discriminable components in order to examine their historical roots and their affiliations with ideas in related fields has been acknowledged as very useful. Now Lovejoy sharply distinguishes the sociology of knowledge from philosophy as the perennial search for truth and wisdom. Philosophy as a normative discipline cannot be content with answering the question, "What is American Philosophy?" solely by historical and cultural analysis. Philosophy must also ask, "What can or should philosophy in America be?" I shall, in order to illustrate and clarify what I take to be Lovejoy's distinction, make some personal observations and draw on reminiscences of my acquaintance with him and his ideas; I beg Lovejoy's and the reader's pardon for indulging in autobiography, but my purpose is to illustrate from my own experience (which must be similar to that of hundreds of other students of American philosophy) the important cultural and philosophical rôle of Lovejoy in American thought.

When the Latin-American philosophers were invited in 1948 to participate in a Pan-American Congress of Philosophy under the auspices of the American Philosophical Association, they were confronted with the question: "Is there a North American Philosophy?" It seemed to me at the time that the Latin-American philosophers were too willing to answer affirmatively so that in their papers they could proceed to show that each Latin-American country had its distinctive philosophy too. When Lovejoy was invited to speak on the question, he declined on the ground that his answer would be simply "No," followed by a perhaps unwanted discourse on the universality of philosophy that rendered the national characteristics of philosophers of secondary importance. He was willing to admit (as I recall the conversation) that pragmatism, in some of its variety of doctrines, might be said to be expressive of certain features of American life and thinking, namely, the emphases on the temporal, pluralistic, experimental, and utilitarian phases of our culture. As philosophers, however, our task is not simply to express such modes of existence but to analyze the doctrines held concerning them.

Lovejoy has in his philosophical writing given much weight to time and dualism in the theory of knowledge. His own theory of knowledge grew out of his intensive study of the ideas of evolutionism, of the great chain of being (especially of its temporalization by Leibniz), and of the *un*critical realisms of William James, Bertrand Russell, and Alfred N. Whitehead. It is a fact that the most thorough historical study of evolutionism and the most critical analysis of pragmatism in the last half century were offered by Lovejoy to American philosophers; but it is, unfortunately, also a fact that these studies have been much ignored. American philosophers have adopted the epistemological views of Bertrand Russell and Alfred N. Whitehead without meeting the critical objections to their theories of perspectives and prehensions so meticulously analyzed by Lovejoy in his *Revolt Against Dualism*, a model of philosophical analysis.

Bertrand Russell (whose right to a professorship at the City College of New York was vigorously defended in 1940 by Lovejoy, M. R. Cohen, John Dewey, W. P. Montague, J. H. Randall, Jr., and practically the whole educational world in the United States) has hardly shown his skill as a logician in his analysis of American pragmatism. In the first place, he does not distinguish among the varieties of pragmatism in any way approaching the discriminations made by Lovejoy in his article of 1908, " The Thirteen Pragmatisms "; and in the second place, he shows little understanding of the liberalism in American philosophy when he finds James's and Dewey's pragmatic theories of truth to be the same as those of the Nazis and Soviet Marxists. Soviet philosophers agree with Russell only on the Nazism.

Russell's eminent countryman and collaborator in mathematical logic, Alfred North Whitehead, after many years of impressive teaching and writing of philosophy at Harvard, became an adopted " American philosopher," thus adding another variety to our list of ambiguities surrounding that term. Now, Whitehead's personal charm and sweet temper and kindly disposition do not condone the obscurity of his metaphysical terms. In *The Revolt Against Dualism* Lovejoy undertook a painstaking analysis of some of these obscurities among objective relativists, including Whitehead's own monistic synthesis, couched in "prehensions" of "organic unities" where everything is related to everything else. The rôle of Lovejoy's poignant criticisms, unheeded unfortunately by American admirers of Whitehead's idealism, has been to warn us of the "metaphysical pathos" into which lovers of obscure monisms tend to fall. William James's radical empiricism and Bergson's intuitionism, whatever share they may have had in the making of Whitehead's metaphysics, would have left a more permanent mark on philosophy in America were it not for Lovejoy's penetrating criticisms.

Ralph Barton Perry, whose *Thought and Character of William James* is a monument of American scholarship on the sources of pragmatism, describes in Jamesian fashion the democratic and religious respect for persons as "characteristically American." Some well-known public figures in America have failed to realize that by attacking the character and reputation of a person whom they suspect to be subversive, without caring too much about due process and the rules of evidence, they are emulating the Communist Party tactics of character assassination and disregard of the individual. Since these public figures are Americans elected by other American citizens, the characteristic imputed to Americans by Perry must be, as I am sure he will grant, an ideal of what we should like Americans to be. And if people everywhere learned to respect persons, there would then be no difference between Americans and other people. The Prussian-born philosopher Immanuel Kant sought to defend such a universal moral ideal in his ethics and cosmopolitan philosophy of history, without having to wait for American philosophy. Evidently, Lovejoy did not follow the advice of his Harvard teacher, William James, that the best way to study Kant was to go around rather than through his philosophy.

Perry's Americanism is not in fact the exclusive property of even democratic thinkers, for every defender of intellectual aristocracy in the history of philosophy from Aristotle to Leibniz and Santayana has defended, as part precisely of the aristocratic code, the respect for persons of which James made so much. Long before the New World was explored and settled by Italian, Spanish, French, Dutch, and British adventurers and slave-traffickers, the religious leaders of Oriental, Greek, Hebrew, and Christian faiths founded morality on respect for the good in persons as creatures of God. Lovejoy in an article on " William James as Philosopher," published in the *International Journal of Ethics* in 1911, the year after James died, hailed James's religious regard for the individual and his creative potentialities as one of the salient characteristics of his philosophy; but Lovejoy noted that this sort of moral individualism appears also in the works of the American poet Whitman—and in the Russian religious mystic Tolstoy.

Having myself been taught philosophy by students and contemporaries of William James, like Harry A. Overstreet, Morris R. Cohen (who, however, preferred Charles S. Peirce's more rigorous pragmaticism to James's psychologism), William P. Montague, Irwin Edman, Stephen C. Pepper, and John Dewey, I early accepted the prevailing notion that there was *a* philosophy called pragmatism that was grass-roots American philosophy. A midwestern philosopher, E. H. Hollands, who came from the University of Kansas to the University of Southern California as Visiting Professor in 1930, first introduced me to the idealistic traditions in America. These not only antedated pragmatism but furnished it with Kantian and Hegelian elements that profoundly modified the empiricism in American thought derived from Bacon, Locke, Berkeley, and Hume. My doctoral dissertation, accordingly, attempted an idealistic critique of experimentalism; fortunately, only part of this was ever published, viz., two chapters on the non-American experimentalists Boyle and Galileo.

It was a Lithuanian-American friend of mine, the late Jerome Rosenthal (whose tragically prolonged illness deprived America of one of the most learned and acute critics of Hegelian and Marxian philosophy) who encouraged me to dig more deeply into the history of experimentalism and the impact of the natural sciences on the American pragmatists. And it was natural for him to recommend to me the erudite writings of Arthur O. Lovejoy on the history of evolutionism and other scientific theories in the history of philosophy. It was this same Jerome Rosenthal who suggested my proposing to Lovejoy in 1938 that we needed in America a journal devoted to the history of philosophy. There was no reply to my letter for several months, and I had given up the idea, not knowing that Lovejoy had gone to Europe as an Emeritus Professor and that the letter was pursuing him all over Europe. When the reply came, it was a very long and detailed one; it was not simply an enthusiastic endorsement of the idea of a historical journal, but a convincing argument that the journal should be more general than the history of philosophy in order to cut across related historical research in literature and the arts, in the sciences, in social and political movements, and in ethical and religious reflection; in short, that we needed a Journal of the History of Ideas.

Lovejoy had already outlined the program for such a journal in his article on " The Historiography of Ideas," in the *Proceedings of the American Philosophical Society* (March, 1938), reprinted in Lovejoy's *Essays in the History of Ideas.* Thus the prospectus of the new Journal was the product of a fusion of Lovejoy's and Rosenthal's ideas. Like the older History of Ideas Club at The Johns Hopkins University, the Journal was motivated by a philosophic need in American thought of becoming more deeply conscious of our intellectual heritage. This became a matter of great cultural urgency in the fall of 1939, when the Nazis invaded Poland, and when Whitehead told us that the United States had become the custodian of Western civilization.

The group of American philosophers and scholars associated with Lovejoy on the Board of Editors of the *Journal of the History of Ideas* (George Boas, Crane Brinton, Gilbert Chinard, Morris R. Cohen, Richard McKeon, Perry Miller, Marjorie Nicolson, John Herman Randall, Jr., and others) were distinguished leaders in their fields who felt the urgency and eagerly supported America's greatest historian of ideas as their Editor-in-Chief. I was more than repaid for my share of doing the work of a managing editor by my association with Lovejoy, whose long, detailed, and very helpful critical comments on manuscripts were a precious correspondence course for me and the authors.

My book on *Evolution and the Founders of Pragmatism* was the outcome of Lovejoy's suggestion that the Harvard liberals at the time of the Darwinian controversy were not only precursors and founders of a variety of pragmatisms but also an important group in the history of American liberalism. This suggestion, coming from America's most astute critic of the pragmatic movement, as John Dewey liked to call it, led me toward the historical roots of the thirteen pragmatisms, roots which I traced to the diverse interests of the founding fathers of the liberal movement in such fields as the methodology of the sciences (Chauncey Wright, William James, and Charles S. Peirce), the philosophy of law (Nicholas St. John Green and Oliver

Wendell Holmes, Jr.), the philosophy of history (John Fiske), and the philosophy of religion (F. E. Abbot's scientific theism and James's will to believe). The point is that I would not have suspected such a rich diversity of ideas in the history of but one school of American philosophy had not Lovejoy shown me that what was so loosely termed " pragmatism " was not one coherent doctrine but, in fact, a whole congeries of ideas. Keeping in mind the distinct tasks of the cultural historian and the philosopher, I have learned, thanks to Lovejoy, to appreciate in the writings of the pragmatic philosophers what ideas they have contributed to philosophy and what inadequacies lurk among them.

There are then two sets of ambiguities in the phrase " American philosophy," one due to the cultural complexity of our social history, the other to the want of clear definition of the problems and method of philosophy. Hence, it should not surprise us, though it may be disillusioning to many, to read the following candid statement by Herbert W. Schneider in his *A History of American Philosophy* (preface, pp. viii-ix):

> The reader of this story will probably be at least as be-wildered as I am in trying to tell what American history teaches us or what American philosophy ' stands for.'

My own experience in tracing the genesis and analyzing the outcome of but one school of American philosophy (which did stand for liberal democratic ideals) also confirms Schneider's statement, as well as Lovejoy's early analysis of the thirteen pragmatisms. If we add to these pragmatisms the idealisms (Berkeleyan and Neoplatonic, the St. Louis Hegelians and the Royceans), realisms (neo-Thomistic, logical, critical), and positivisms (Johnson, Stallo, Bridgman, the Viennese and Warsaw schools), without counting the phenomenologists, sociologists of knowledge, Marxists, Humanists, Personalists, Existentialists,

Theosophists, and what not else, all on the American philosophical scene, we can better still appreciate the force of Schneider's informed observation. The democratic ethos of "live and let live" has surely spawned a fascinating and odd variety of philosophies in America, and none but a spiritual totalitarianism would wish to destroy the freedom to create a diversity of ways of thinking on ultimate questions. The only sort of philosophy we cannot with impunity tolerate in the defense of liberal traditions of American thought is the totalitarian monolithic authoritarianism that would block the road to inquiry, as Peirce put it, and would forget that it is through the individual's effort that the inevitable comes to pass, as Justice Holmes put it.

One great lesson we can learn from the history of American or any other philosophy is that great philosophers do not merely "reflect" prevalent social forces (as Marxists dogmatically claim), but react critically to historically grounded but often unreflectively held and inadequate beliefs. I recall that soon after World War II Lovejoy urged the need for more public forums and discussion groups on Marxism, led by those who were trained in the critical habits of historical research in order to counter the distortion of historical and philosophical truth by Communist Party propagandists, busy organizing "front" forums and clandestine meetings. The historian should also be able to teach the dangers of permitting the crude tactics of crushing one sort of totalitarianism by installing another, as happened in Germany with the advent of Hitler. Lovejoy's vigorous opposition to both Nazi and Stalinist totalitarianisms is a high example of the union of disinterested love of truth with deep human concern for the preservation of intellectual and political freedom.

American philosophy can be regarded as the testing ground of liberal ideals of intellectual freedom and human welfare. It can stand that test successfully only by carrying on the ancient liberal tradition of the pursuit of reason in the arts, the sciences, and the conduct of life. It must do more. It must press the pursuit beyond residual dogmas of class, creed, and nationalism whenever they interfere with the free life of the mind. That there are such residual dogmas, challenging enough to the philosopher in America, history and our own time more than amply show. In order to win this battle for freedom, he will need Lovejovian courage and wisdom.

DOROTHY STIMSON

The History of Ideas Club

ꜱꜱꜱꜱꜱꜱꜱꜱꜱꜱꜱꜱꜱꜱꜱꜱꜱꜱꜱꜱꜱ

The First World War marks for many people the end of one epoch and the beginning of another. For Johns Hopkins University it indicated the completion of the institution's first forty years; professors of its early years were passing from the classrooms and younger men with fresh ideas and different methods were taking their places.

Such changes were inevitable, aside from the passage of time, for the first quarter of the twentieth century registered a decided shift in emphasis from what was coming to be spoken of as "mere" erudition—the grammarian's minutiae and the historian's preoccupation with dates and politics—to a renewed realization of the oneness of thought, the importance of values, of culture, of underlying forces shaping human affairs. Not least of these forces was the potency of scientific ideas. The theory of relativity had begun to crack the mold of century-old physical and philosophical systems just as the automobile, the airplane, and the motion pictures were already changing the patterns of society. John Dewey was in the full tide of his pragmatic philosophy and its application to education in a twentieth century democracy, while James Harvey Robinson and his colleagues were guiding hundreds of students in the paths of the "new history." Dr. Flexner's appraisal of medical education in 1910 had started a beneficent revolution in the medical

174

schools. Education at all levels was increasingly under discussion, for revolution was stalking through the halls of scholarship as well as through old established governments and civilizations.

What were the forces underlying these movements? Were the ideals, the standards, the methods of the nineteenth century no longer valid? What trends could one discover in the past and the present that might suggest the course of the future? The scholar's accumulation of accurate texts and the careful analysis of their contents, though still fundamental, now seemed an insufficient guide to the questioning minds in the twentieth century classrooms. Something more was needed. The past needed reinterpretation in the light of a stormy present, and the younger professors realized it.

A leader among these new men at Johns Hopkins University was Dr. Arthur O. Lovejoy, who had been appointed professor of philosophy in 1910, at the age of thirty-seven. At the close of the First World War, as one means of dealing with the new conceptions, Dr. Lovejoy had recourse to a monthly discussion club for the encouragement of research and for the consideration of ideas by scholars of varied interests.

Even before seminars and courses had been started at the University, such clubs and societies had been encouraged by President Gilman, as a stimulus to research and as a means of drawing together workers in kindred fields. Dr. John C. French in his *History of the University Founded by Johns Hopkins* (1946) records that in the course of time some of these early organizations had merged into departmental seminars while others had been superseded by the rise of inter-university societies like the Modern Language Association. All except the Philological Association, the first one to be founded (1877) and still in existence today, had died away before Dr. Lovejoy organized the History of Ideas Club. Since it is not mentioned in the official *History*, a record of the Club's early years should be preserved while memories are fresh.

The exact origins of the History of Ideas Club and its reasons for being do not seem to have been recorded. One member recalls that it grew out of a conversation over the lunch table by Professors Lovejoy, Gilbert Chinard, and George Boas. The earliest existing record, the minutes of a meeting held January 24, 1923, refers to a previous meeting, that of May 5, 1922, of which no trace remains. But one can to a certain extent reconstruct the situation out of which the Club grew, with the aid of one or two bits of evidence from later records. Its active organizers were with one outstanding exception from the younger, more recent appointees to the Hopkins faculty, men who had had the major part of their academic training in other parts of the United States. Dr. Lovejoy himself, after study at California, Harvard, and a year in Paris, had taught for some years at universities in the far and middle west. He had arrived in Baltimore not long before the outbreak of the First World War had seized the country and the University in its grip. Until that grip was broken by the return of peace, professors could give little time and attention to a forum for scholarly discussion.

The sound scholarship of the German universities of the mid-nineteenth century was, as is well known, basic at the Johns Hopkins University. One of its leading exponents there, Professor James W. Bright, an authority on English philology, was also alive to the new currents of thought. Under his aegis, gratefully remembered to this day, Professor Lovejoy and his associates organized their new club. Professor Bright was its president until declining health compelled his resignation. The Club's resolutions, proposed after his death in 1926, indicate how well he had served during that postwar period of transition:

. . . Professor Bright was known to the learned world chiefly as a grammarian and as an editor of texts. His students and his colleagues, however, knew that his interests were much wider in scope. In truth, he must be called a philologist in the classical sense of that term. . . . As time went on, his emphasis upon the literary side of philological study grew ever more pronounced. In his later years what may be called intellectual history came to be the chief concern of philologists everywhere, and nowadays the kind of study which this Club stands for is central and dominant in philological circles. . . . It is characteristic of him that he should be among the organizers of the History of Ideas Club and its first president. . . .

> Respectfully submitted,
> Gilbert Chinard
> Kemp Malone
> Committee

In accepting these resolutions at its meeting on January 18, 1927, the Club also registered that a change in the directions of scholarly thought had been the inspiration of its own existence. As one reads the first minutes of the Club, one realizes that it was the newcomers, the younger scholars, on the faculty who actually organized and ran the Club, giving it the character which it has maintained to this day. Perhaps it was the presidency of the elderly scholar-grammarian that gave the Club prestige at the outset; but one wonders, not without oral confirmation from some of its members, whether a little of the spirit of revolt against grammatical erudition alone had not actuated those original members.

The oldest record remaining reads as follows:

The Club met at 4 P. M., January 24, 1923, in 113 Gilman Hall. There were nineteen members present. The minutes of the meeting of May 5, 1922 were read by Professor [David M.] Robinson and approved. Dr. [George] Boas then read a paper on a phase of Traditionalism from the attempted refutation of Condillac's theory of the origin of language by Rousseau to the condemnation of Bonetty by Pope Pius IX.

A synopsis of the paper follows and a record of the discussion, Dr. Boas serving both as speaker and as acting-secretary.

At the next meeting, on March 1st, Professor Lovejoy gave the report for the Committee on Organization and Program. He was its chairman, with Professors H. Carrington Lancaster and David M. Robinson as the other members. Both of these men were among the newcomers to the University, Professor Lancaster having arrived in 1919 and Professor Robinson in 1915. Incidentally, who had appointed this committee, and when? The minutes do not say. The " brief constitution " they presented, which was approved at this meeting, first named the Club, then stated:

Section 2: The purposes of the society are those set forth in the call for the first meeting, viz., to bring together members of the University for the occasional presentation and discussion of papers and informal communications in the field of the " history of ideas," *i. e.*, the historical study of the development and influence of general philosophical conceptions, ethical ideas, and esthetic fashions, in occi-' dental literature, and of the relations of these to manifestations of the same ideas and tendencies in the history of philosophy, of science, and of political and social movements. The organization is based upon the belief that in the field indicated topics of common interest to representatives of diverse specialties will be found, and that the existence of such a society may perhaps promote a useful cross-fertilization of the work of the several historical and humanistic departments.

Those who know Professor Lovejoy's work will recognize here his ideas and his style.

The Club has faithfully carried out these purposes throughout the years, contributing through its vigorous discussions to the cross-fertilization of ideas. The limitation to "occidental literature" marked out its field in 1923 from that of the Philological Society; but as time passed, this restriction ceased to be remembered. When the constitution was reviewed in 1950, at the November 9 meeting, Professor Lancaster moved an amendment adding to the original phrase the words "and oriental," with the comment that "the reasons for the original restriction to occidental literature no longer existed." Without discussion the change was unanimously adopted.

The categories of membership listed in the third section of the constitution provided for: 1. "Teachers or other officers of the Philosophical Faculty of the University" who wished to belong; * 2. Graduate students recommended by their professors; 3. "Other persons invited on recommendation of its Committee on Program and Membership." Forty-four names were on the secretary's record of that 1923 meeting as members of the Club. In actual practice membership in the Club was a simple matter: one might attend a meeting with a friend to hear a particular speaker, become interested enough to ask the secretary to send a postcard notice of the next meeting and pay a quarter to cover the costs of notification. Almost from the outset, for example, members of the Goucher College faculty have been participants, to their own great intellectual enjoyment. Men and women no longer actively engaged in academic respects have also attended, thereby continuing their scholarly interests, and occasionally enlivening the discussions with their comments and queries.

The constitution provided in section 4 for the simplest organi-

---

* A penciled comment in the margin of Dr. Lovejoy's copy of this document reads: "This includes the scientists, I understand." But one wonders about the professors in the Medical School.

zation possible: "a president, a secretary (both of whom shall be members of the Philosophical Faculty of the Johns Hopkins University) and a Committee on Program and Membership, consisting of the President and Secretary and two others." They were to be elected annually; but no president was to be eligible for more than two consecutive terms. Dues were not mentioned. Not until November 9, 1950, was the constitution amended to have the secretary act as treasurer also and submit an annual report. At the same time annual dues were set at fifty cents. The treasurer's report for 1950-51 showed a paid-up membership of sixty-three people.

The original scheme for six meetings a year has continued unchanged. "Communications" were to be not more than thirty-five or forty minutes long; but when the time of the meetings was shifted almost at once from the noon hour to the evening, papers were permitted to be fifty minutes in length. This fifth section of the constitution also provided that speakers should furnish the secretary with brief extracts for incorporation in the minutes—unfortunately a rule too often disregarded, thereby making the secretary's task an onerous one.

Some secretaries rose brilliantly to the challenge. Their minutes of papers and discussions still make fascinating reading. The reports made by Professors Boas, Kemp Malone and, much later, by Victor Lowe are particularly interesting. Other secretaries were content to record the bare facts of the meeting, the number present and the number and sometimes the names of those participating in the discussion. If the speaker provided a synopsis, it was usually but not always appended. Occasionally speakers talked without notes, with varying degrees of success. Professor Charles A. Beard's talk on historiography in 1935 is remembered with disappointment; on the other hand, Dean Ames's presentation, in 1926, of the history of the concept of light is still spoken of as a masterpiece of oral scholarship. So also was his discussion on a half century of American education, made in 1935 just before his retirement from the presidency of the University, an address not reported at his request but not yet forgotten.

On January 18, 1927, Dr. William H. Welch spoke to the Club. Then in his late seventies, Dr. Welch was just embarking on his new career as professor of the history of medicine at the Johns Hopkins Medical School. Since 1884 he had been professor of pathology, then Director of the School of Hygiene and Public Health. Now he was bringing his wit, his wisdom and his profound and broad knowledge to the organization and development of the Institute of the History of Medicine, one of the loves of his rich life. From the fullness of his knowledge Dr. Welch spoke without notes to that crowded meeting. As Professor Kemp Malone, then secretary, has caught in his minutes of this occasion not only some of Dr. Welch's charm but also indications of the range, the allusiveness and the penetration of the discussion that followed admirably exemplifying these meetings at their best, the minutes of this talk and of the ensuing discussion are here reproduced.

January 18, 1927

. . . Dr. William H. Welch . . . talked informally on the part which erroneous hypothesis has played in the advancement of knowledge, with particular reference to the history of medicine. The speaker began by reading a quotation from an author whose name the secretary did not catch, since he is unfamiliar with it. The quotation set forth the idea that a false hypothesis is frequently more stimulating and hence more fruitful than a true hypothesis; as illustration Empedocles's theory of the Four Elements was contrasted with Democritus's atomic theory. The theory of Empedocles, though false, proved the starting-point for modern chemistry, which still operates with elements, though they are not the same as those of Empedocles. The speaker went on to point out that Hippocrates, the father of medicine, was likewise a follower of Empedocles, and built up on the Four Elements his own theory of the Four Humors, a conception which dominated medicine until well into modern times. By way of further illustration the speaker told of Servetus's discovery of pulmonary circulation of the blood, a discovery which grew out of an interest in determining how the so-called animal spirits could be formed in the brain from the vital spirits in the pneuma.

Reverting to Greek Medicine, the speaker began with the observation that from the days of Hippocrates, at least, there had been two streams in medicine: the natural and the superstitious. Miraculous cures gave rise to what we now call psycho-therapy, a scientifically sound and important branch of medicine. Psycho-therapy was well understood by the Greeks, and very successfully practiced in the Greek temples, which had the function now fulfilled by sanatoriums and the like. Greek psycho-therapy grew out of an earlier miraculous healing in sacred places, hence the connection with temples. The speaker compared the cures worked at Lourdes, the efficacy of the so-called king's touch, and the value of Christian Science treatment in many cases. The scientific principle involved is the influence of mental states on the health of the body. Another branch of superstitious medicine is the so-called signature symbolism. The notion was widespread that cures could be made by applying like to like: yellow things would cure jaundice, red things would stop hemorrhages, etc. The search for things with such curative properties led to not a few valuable additions to the pharmacopoea. Similarly, astrology led to astronomy, and alchemy to chemistry and physics.

Superstitious medicine has existed from the earliest times, said the speaker further, but natural medicine, in the western world at least, was founded by Hippocrates. Hippocrates believed that all disease had a natural cause; he did not operate with spirits, bewitchings and the like. The basis of his pathology was the Four Humors, disturbances in which produced disease. These disturbances were caused by the so-called *materies morbi*, which entered from without, especially from the air. This theory of the spread of disease is known as miasm. The miasmic disturbances were combated by Nature herself, who would usually work a cure if let alone. The function of the physician was to assist Nature. Nature's method was that of coction, or expulsion of the trouble-making elements. Hence the physician must help Nature out by stimulating the processes of excretion. Hippocrates taught that by a study of the activities of the body the healing process could be observed and the physician could see when the moment for his intervention was at hand. This doctrine led to the practice of watching the patient carefully, describing symptoms, and distinguishing the various diseases one from another. The theory of coction was exploded in the 17th century, by the introduction of the cinchona bark, which cured without any expulsion of trouble-making matter. The theory that the body itself fights disease, however, has endured to this day, and is fundamental in medical practice.

The theory of miasm was from the beginning opposed to that of contagion. Belief in miasm led to a high development of sanitation and care for public health in ancient times, and miasm furnished the theoretical basis for the British Public Health Act of 1848, the piece of legislation which led to all modern government regulation in the field of sanitation. Modern science has shown that contagion, not miasm, is the proper explanation of the great pestilences, but the contrary belief has been very helpful in promoting sanitation and thus improving the health and comfort of the people.

The speaker concluded by remarking that it is sometimes fortunate that no hypothesis at all is advanced. In the 18th century a cure for scurvy, and the method of vaccination to forestall smallpox, were discovered, but this did not lead to any generalizations for 100 years or more, and it was just as well, since in the state of science at that day any generalization would in all likelihood have been wrong. This led the speaker to a generalization of his own, to the effect that in the biological field the hypothesis nearly always turned out to be wrong, because of the enormous complexity of the biological processes, and the number of factors which could not be captured.

The paper was then thrown open for discussion. Mr. Havens opened the discussion by quoting from Chaucer a satirical passage on the medical art. This reminded the speaker of the attacks on Hippocrates and his followers by the rival school of medicine: Hippocrates was described as meditating on death, when he ought to be busy doing something for his patient. Letting Nature do the work, according to this view, was equivalent to deserting the patient. There followed a good deal of talk about semantics, the planets, Planck's quantum theory, Bohr, and Bergson, which the secretary finds hard to report adequately, and so omits.

Mr. Boas then asked why the speaker included in the title of his talk the word "erroneous." The speaker at once replied that the word was probably superfluous, since at bottom all hypotheses are erroneous; his terminology was a concession to common sense. Mr. Boas proceeded to argue that only the true part of the hypothesis had influence, so that the false part could be set aside. This led to a one-sided dialectic which the secretary refuses to report. Mr. Lancaster interposed with an analysis of the psychology of cures by the king's touch and the like. He said that if the patient understood that there was no virtue in the king's touch as such, and it was the patient's faith in it which made him whole, then the patient would not be able to muster up the needed faith and the cure would fail. Here then the false part of the hypothesis had a decided influence. The speaker agreed.

Prompted by some question which the secretary failed to note, the speaker now sketched for us the study of the introduction of anesthesia into surgical practice. Starting with Sir Humphry Davy, at the end of the 18th century, he came down through the " laughing gas " drunks, Long, and Wells, to Morton and Jackson, and Morton's famous operation of October 14, 1846. He asked the Club to vote on the question of the man best entitled to be called the discoverer of the method, but somehow the question never came to a vote. The speaker indicated clearly he would have plumped for Morton. Mr. Chinard favored Long and Mr. Miller upheld the claims of Davy. Mr. Lancaster tried to carry the method further back, by quoting from a 16th century French poem, *La Semaine,* by Du Bartas, according to which God put Adam to sleep with a cooling draught, as skilful surgeons do, before extracting his rib to make Eve with. But the speaker made the point that the old surgeons used opiates, alcohol and the like freely to reduce the sufferings of their patients. The discussion then shifted back to the claims of Long and Morton; the importance of publication in establishing priority was brought out.

Mr. Chinard brought the discussion back to its starting point by offering a linguistic parallel to the medical testimony. He pointed out that in the 18th century all sorts of absurd theories were afloat about the origins of the various European languages: they were derived from Hebrew, Greek, Celtic among others. These theories led to comparisons of the various languages concerned, and eventually, after the discovery of Sanskrit, the true relationship of the Indo-European languages was worked out. The speaker added the Wasserman test as an example of a false theory which led to something valuable. He summed up by saying that he was not claiming to have advanced an original or even a paradoxical conception of the value of scientific hypothesis. He was inclined to believe that Mr. Boas was right in his view of the whole matter. But perhaps there was something in what he said, and in any case the subject was interesting and the discussion had been amusing.

With this the discussion ended and the meeting was adjourned.

Respectfully submitted,

Kemp Malone
Secretary

The setting for these Club meetings has varied. Started in one of the classrooms of Gilman Hall, they were soon moved to the faculty lounge, then in Carroll Mansion. When that building became an administrative center the Club shifted back to a large seminar room in Gilman. There for some twenty-odd years the Club exemplified high thinking and hard sitting for two long hours on the second Thursday of six months during each academic year. Two long tables, end to end, ran the length of the room. Eight or ten low-backed oak armchairs were ranged along the sides of the tables, with two at one end for the president and the speaker of the evening. The secretary sat at the president's left and Professor Lovejoy usually in his accustomed seat at the speaker's right. Graduate students and guests mingled with faculty members on hard classroom chairs ranged often two deep around three walls of the room, leaving the seats at the table for the leading professors and an occasional bold soul who joined those pundits. Forty or more men and women could find places there under the high drafty windows or pressed back against the long black-boarded walls. When sixty or seventy tried to squeeze their way in, the meeting would have to be adjourned to a larger space. Usually though, late-comers could be fitted into the classroom, there to sit in the smoke-filled air listening with more or less interest to a scholarly paper read often nervously by even the most experienced and renowned scholars. Then they would resettle themselves in the stiff chairs eagerly to await the opening of the discussion. What would Professor Lovejoy say? A comment, a question from him and the debate would begin. Other professors would join in and an occasional remark would be made by someone on the sidelines. At ten o'clock the meeting adjourned. As the group streamed through the corridors, one could overhear such comments as "He never really answered ——'s argument." "That was a good point he made about . . . ." That audience, however silent it had been, was not asleep.

Since the fall of 1951 the meetings of the Club have usually been held in the Goodwillie Room in Gilman Hall. The long tables are there, but the many deep lounge chairs, pre-empted by the first comers, may perhaps deaden the critical faculties of the listeners and the size of the room may lessen the sense of intimacy in the discussion—or is it that Professor Lovejoy now is less often in attendance?—but the tradition of discussion and debate remains, for this has been and still is a true forum for the consideration of ideas.

When in 1948 Professor Lovejoy attained his seventy-fifth birthday, the *Journal of the History of Ideas* carried a series of articles in his honor. In one of these, "A. O. Lovejoy as Teacher," Miss Marjorie Nicolson, herself now professor of English on the graduate faculty of Columbia University, wrote:

> Professor Lovejoy—conditioned by Baltimore, I still think of him so—has changed little in a quarter of a century. Perhaps his Prussian-cut hair and goatee are whiter, though they were iron-gray even in 1923. His speech is as clipped and precise (and frequently as devastating) today as when I first heard him. His eyes are still the blue steel that pierced through my youthful shallow ignorance and arrogance on the occasion when I first ventured a remark in his seminar—which was not early in the term, I assure you . . . .

At times when Professor Lovejoy himself was the main speaker the Club meetings might seem an extension of the seminar room; for, as in the seminar,

> . . . he came with those piles of manila envelopes we all remember [Miss Nicolson is speaking again] from which he would draw forth half-sheets of paper covered with his sprawling writing (which . . . still shows what chirographers call " the slant of optimism "). In those envelopes were the skeletons of books and articles he has since published and of others for which we are still waiting. Usually he began by reading from his notes, though they never served for more than a point of departure and a source for illustrations, as he went on amplifying his theme from the richness of his learning in many languages and an astonishing breadth of encyclopedic knowledge . . . .

Those interested in Professor Lovejoy's outlook and method, the basis of the Club as well as of his seminars, should read at least the first chapter on " The Study of the History of Ideas " in his *The Great Chain of Being* (1936). Many articles by Professor Lovejoy have been published in learned journals. Some of these articles have been reissued in a volume, *Essays in the History of Ideas* (1948), at the initiative of the History of Ideas Club in celebration of the author's birthday, as well as in recognition of the twenty-fifth anniversary of the Club. In the Foreword, Professor Don Cameron Allen, one of the committee in charge of publication, paid tribute to the Club as " a sort of seminar where mature men and women learned new and valuable lessons," and attributed the importance of the Club " to the genius of Professor Lovejoy, who is not only the father of the Club but also the chief inspirer of the modern study of the history of ideas . . . . That we have this new insight is largely the work of Professor Lovejoy, who brought to this wavering and unfruitful study an amazing practice of analysis, a special feeling for terminology, and a careful ritual of self-examination that protects the student from his inherent narrowness, from his own emotional weaknesses." Not only has philosophy profited but the study of literature and art has gained " in range and vitality." Indeed, the present students of the humanities owe a debt to Professor Lovejoy's teaching and his influence of which Professor Allen thinks many may not be aware, so thoroughly has his work been accepted and become a part of this age's " climate of ideas." Thinking of this type was at the core of the Club's activities.

Sponsorship of the *Essays* was voted by the Club, January 9, 1947, during the presidency of Professor Havens. He appointed as the committee of editors, Professor Ludwig Edelstein, Chairman, Professor Boas and Professor Allen. Eighteen months later the *Essays* were published. It should be noted that the idea had originated with Professor Edelstein, since the minutes do not record that fact. Encouraged by the success of this venture, the Club approved on January 12, 1950, the appointment of a committee to study further plans. Finally, on February 14, 1952, announcement was made that a brief history of the Club would be prepared by one of its members, to be published " together with one or more suitable essays on intellectual history."

For three decades the History of Ideas Club has pursued its steady course through days of inflation, depression and global cataclysm. Only once, seemingly, has the Club wavered in its steady progress, though no one now remembers why. The minutes of April 9, 1936, record that a special meeting was to be held on April 16 " to discuss future policy and to improve the present conditions of the organization." Eighteen members were present on the sixteenth. The president, Professor Kent Roberts Greenfield, asked for suggestions to increase interest in the study of the history of ideas. According to the record, eight members participated in the discussion. The main issue reported in the minutes was whether or not to restrict attendance at the meetings and make them more exclusive. No arguments were recorded. Three resolutions concluded the discussion: 1, Not to resort to principles of selection; 2, To have some papers on the history of medicine; and 3, To consider the publication of a Club journal as soon as feasible.

One clue to a possible explanation of this special meeting lies in the minutes of the meeting on March 19, six weeks earlier: only sixteen people had been present then to hear a paper presented by Professor Lancaster. Usually forty or more were in attendance. While some slip in the notification of the members went far to explain the small number at that particular meeting, still, throughout that winter a decline in attendance had been marked and had aroused fears about the continued usefulness of a club of this nature. Possibly unrest in the University was also a factor. The years of depression had taken their cumulative toll: changes were afoot, shifts in the Faculty were being made, some prominent professors had accepted posts elsewhere. But the usual number had attended the regular April meeting immediately preceding this special one, and there was every indication that the Club would continue to be of service.

This special meeting is only an incident in the Club's history, completely forgotten now even by those who were named as participants in the discussion. According to the minutes, the value of the Club's meetings had not even been questioned. Professor Lovejoy's conviction expressed there that attendance should not be restricted in any way had been supported by the others present, and this policy established at the beginning has been steadily maintained ever since.

The third of the resolutions passed by this special meeting is of particular interest, for it is the sole reference in the still existing minutes of the Club to the possible publication of a Club journal. Unfortunately, the minutes for the final meeting in 1932-33 are missing, as are all minutes for the two years 1933-35, with the exception of a brief memorandum of the final meeting, April 11, 1936. Whether the idea of a journal had been broached at any Club meeting prior to April, 1936, is not now susceptible of proof.

The absence of any later reference to such a project indicates that leading members of the Club realized its own financial inability for such an ambitious undertaking. Professor Lovejoy was undeterred, however, and three years later on November 9, 1939, he announced to the Club the institution of the *Journal of the History of Ideas*. The publication of his *The Great Chain of Being* in 1936 had inspired a reader of its notable first chapter to urge its author to establish a journal and had then secured gifts to a sustaining fund which, with grants from other sources, had enabled Professor Lovejoy and his board of editors to issue volume I in 1939. The *Journal*, like the Club, has gone steadily on its independent way ever since—both institutions being substantial evidence of Dr. Lovejoy's great contributions to the advancement of knowledge. While the *Journal* cannot be claimed as a direct result of the Club's activities, it is unquestionably an outgrowth of the interest and discussion generated by the Club under his inspiration. It has also served to give wider publicity to some of the papers read before the Club.

Obviously one man alone cannot make a club nor carry one on single-handedly for thirty years of fruitful history. From the Club's first days, Professor George Boas has been an invaluable aid. He had joined the University in 1921, becoming in 1933 professor of the history of philosophy. Not only did he read the " communication " presented at the first recorded meeting where he also served as secretary, but time and again his name appears, as secretary for the first few years, as president, as speaker on many occasions and as a frequent participant in the discussions. His energy, his wit and his good sense have been useful in keeping the Club machinery working while his philosophic and aesthetic interests advanced its major purposes.

Reference to the lists of presidents and secretaries (see Appendix A) will show to any one familiar with the scholarly world that other men of varied and notable attainments have also served the Club for longer or shorter periods. For the past ten years the presidents have not succeeded themselves for the one permissible second year, but whoever was secretary by frequent re-election has usually provided the continuity in office that helps administrative machinery to run smoothly. Few others could equal George Boas or Kemp Malone as secretaries, however, for with wit and wisdom as well as broad knowledge they summarized speeches and kept track of elusive and allusive discussions. Their minutes are no bare record but a *jeu d'esprit* in themselves.

The officers with two or three other members as a program committee have invited speakers to address the Club, usually on subjects of their own choosing. Once or twice each year a scholar from another university or some distinguished foreign scholar visiting Johns Hopkins has spoken to the Club, thus serving the wide range of the Club's interests and checking any tendency toward inbreeding. Unfortunately, a complete list of these speakers and their subjects cannot be presented because of the missing minutes for 1933–35. From other sources a few names, dates and general topics have been assembled but gaps still remain (see Appendix B). Nor is it feasible to indicate how many of these speeches have been printed. Some were to become chapters in forthcoming books; others have appeared in learned journals here and abroad, while still others remain in manuscript.

Actually, far more important to the speaker than publication has been the challenge of the invitation to address the Club— to clarify and focus his ideas on a given subject for the consideration of a scholarly mature group of unquestioned intellectual and critical acumen. Small wonder, then, that work hammered out and delivered before such an audience should later be revised and published. This procedure certainly holds true for most of the papers presented by the younger scholars.

A glance down the list of speakers and their topics shows the enrichment of the Club's intellectual fare by the coming of notable scholars to one or another of the Faculties of the University. It also shows how the newcomer was introduced by way of a " communication " to the community of scholars there. Dr. Welch's successor at the Institute of the History of Medicine, Dr. Henry E. Sigerist, addressed the Club in December of his first year at the University. In similar fashion Professors Greenlaw and Spencer were welcomed, as well as many others. The list also reveals another development as the years passed: the enrichment of American scholarship through the impoverishment of European learning in the totalitarian states, as distinguished men found refuge in this country from dictatorship in their own lands. Some of the foreign names on the list, together with the dates on which they gave their addresses, reflect all too clearly political events in Europe; as, for example, Professor Salinas from Spain, Professor Spitzer and Professor Edelstein from Germany, and Professor Engel-Janosi from Austria. What was Europe's loss became America's gain.

Then, too, the Club has provided a common meeting-place for men of science with men of letters. Astronomers, mathematicians, geologists, physicists, and biologists as well as physicians have all from time to time presented papers. Usually some of them attend the meetings regularly, on occasion joining in the discussion. Thus the originally stated purpose of the Club is being fulfilled as discussions range over the history of ideas, whether in politics, in science, or in literature and philosophy. It also enables men from widely separated divisions of the University to become better acquainted with each others' ways of thought. In this age of sharp specialization, such services are valuable in lessening the gap between science and the humanities.

Furthermore, the subjects discussed and the phrasing of their titles reflect on occasion contemporary problems in the world outside the University: "The Historical Meaning of the American Doctrine of Isolation," "Planned Economy in the Eighteenth Century," "The Effect of Conscription on Modern European History," "Geographical Doctrines in Politics," "The Origin and Recent Development of Revolutionary Ideas in China." Is it not significant that these topics are to be found in the discussions of the last ten or fifteen years? "Primitivism," a much discussed subject in the twenties, has yielded place in the forties and fifties to the more vital concerns of revolution in the Far East and of the treatment of capitalism not alone by historians.

Current crises in the University and in the educational world at large are also reflected. One wonders what President Ames said when he reviewed the fifty years of the University without allowing his remarks to be reported. In one of the most difficult years of World War II, Professor Painter for the humanities and Dr. Sigerist for the medical sciences discussed the problems facing university education. That March, Dr. Scott Buchanan faced a crowded room as he discussed the crisis of liberal education and St. John's endeavor to re-shape its curriculum to meet contemporary needs from the recorded wisdom of the ages.

In the main, however, no matter how the topics were phrased

the speakers have presented the results of their own research whether in the records of antiquity or in the present.

A skeptic might inquire, what has all this talk for thirty years actually accomplished? Has the Club *done* anything? Specifically, a book of Dr. Lovejoy's collected essays stands on library shelves because the Club under the leadership of Professor Edelstein had those essays Dr. Lovejoy selected reissued. The Club was not directly responsible for the publication of *The Great Chain of Being*, perhaps the most notable of Dr. Lovejoy's books, nor for the founding of *The Journal of the History of Ideas*. But it would be difficult to prove, or indeed to disprove, that the Club's discussions had not influenced Professor Lovejoy's thinking while providing him with a testing-ground for his ideas even as he was stimulating its members to keener criticism and greater clarity of thought. Nor can the Club point to a long list of published articles and claim direct credit for these contributions to knowledge. Yet one can argue that some at least of these articles might not even have been written had not their authors responded to the invitation to address the Club.

More positively, what the Club has accomplished through these thirty years is a rare and rather subtle service, difficult to define in many words but consciously felt by scores of participants in its sessions. It has provided a forum for the testing of ideas, a forum comprised of mature men and women, most of them on college and university faculties, who by reason of their somewhat isolated positions do not often experience the opportunity of informed debate with their intellectual equals. Before such a forum as the Club, the acknowledged scholar and expert is on his mettle. Woe betide him if he shows evidence of shallow thinking, of illogical argument, of seeming disregard or inadequate appreciation of contradictory evidence. Someone during the discussion following his paper is sure to ask a question pointed at the weak spot. Fallacious thinking will get short shrift. Evidence ignored or neglected may be submitted by the scholars present possibly from the speaker's own field or from a related one. The speaker is indeed being tested by his peers. Such an experience is a salutary one for all concerned. The younger scholar realizes again that authorities are not infallible, that the advancement of knowledge is the product of many men's work, and that valid criticism generously given is a great boon. The interchange of idea and argument is a delight to intellectually alive people. Those who have not experienced it can hardly realize what exhilaration and refreshment can come from such a battle of the wits even when one is only a bystander. Who can measure the exact extent and value of such an interchange?

Members of the Club in past years look back upon its meetings with unstinted pleasure. As one wrote: "It is just the sort of intellectual activity that should take place on a university campus, an example of cross-fertilization in scholarly fields, a testing-ground for anyone with ideas to present (especially with Mr. Lovejoy sitting there with his prodigious knowledge and his extraordinary critical activities) and a delight for any one who can enjoy mental activity."

After thirty years the pattern of provocative papers and free, candid discussion is now well set, though the participants shift as the years pass. It may well be that in a later history of the Johns Hopkins University, the History of Ideas Club, the creation of Professor Lovejoy and his coworkers, will stand out as a most influential activity in having exemplified during these decades the true function of a university, the pursuit of truth and the advancement of knowledge.

Officers of the History of Ideas Club

▷▷▷▷▷▷▷▷▷▷▷▷▷▷▷▷▷▷▷▷▷▷

May 5, 1922	Minutes (missing) read by Professor Robinson on January 24, 1923
January 24, 1923	*President*: not named, probably Professor Bright *Secretary*: George Boas *Committee on Organization*: Professors Lovejoy, Lancaster, Robinson
1923–24	*President*: James W. Bright *Secretary*: George Boas (on leave), George W. Small
1924–25	*President*: James W. Bright *Secretary*: George Boas
1925–26	*President*: Gilbert Chinard *Secretary*: George Boas
1926–27	*President*: Gilbert Chinard *Secretary*: Lois Whitney (resigned). Kemp Malone
1927–28	*President*: Arthur O. Lovejoy *Secretary*: Kemp Malone
1928–29	*President*: Arthur O. Lovejoy *Secretary*: James Hart
1929–30	*President*: Henry C. Lancaster *Secretary*: Hazelton Spencer

Appendix A

1930–31	*President*:	Henry C. Lancaster
	Secretary:	Raymond P. Hawes
1931–32	*President*:	Kemp Malone
	Secretary:	Ernst Feise
1932–33	*President*:	Kemp Malone
	Secretary:	Ernst Feise
1933–34	*President*:	George Boas
	Secretary:	David R. McKee (?)
1934–35	*President*:	George Boas
	Secretary:	David R. McKee
1935–36	*President*:	Kent Roberts Greenfield
	Secretary:	Harold Cherniss
1936–37	*President*:	Kent Roberts Greenfield
	Secretary:	Sanford P. Larkey
1937–38	*President*:	Hazelton Spencer
	Secretary:	Sanford P. Larkey
1938–39	*President*:	Arthur O. Lovejoy
	Secretary:	Sanford P. Larkey
1939–40	*President*:	W. Stull Holt
	Secretary:	Harold Cherniss
1940–41	*President*:	Fred K. Lane
	Secretary:	Ludwig Edelstein
1941–42	*President*:	Emile Malakis
	Secretary:	Ludwig Edelstein
1942–43	*President*:	Henry E. Sigerist
	Secretary:	Ludwig Edelstein

Officers of the History of Ideas Club

| 1943–44 | *President:* | Ernst Feise |
| | *Secretary:* | Ludwig Edelstein |

| 1944–45 | *President:* | Ludwig Edelstein |
| | *Secretary:* | Clara P. McMahon |

| 1945–46 | *President:* | Sidney Painter |
| | *Secretary:* | Clara P. McMahon |

| 1946–47 | *President:* | Raymond D. Havens |
| | *Secretary:* | Clara P. McMahon |

| 1947–48 | *President:* | Leo Spitzer |
| | *Secretary:* | Clara P. McMahon |

| 1948–49 | *President:* | Owsei Temkin |
| | *Secretary:* | Clara P. McMahon |

| 1949–50 | *President:* | Henry C. Lancaster |
| | *Secretary:* | Victor A. Lowe |

| 1950–51 | *President:* | H. Bentley Glass |
| | *Secretary:* | Victor A. Lowe |

| 1951–52 | *President:* | Fritz Machlup |
| | *Secretary:* | Bruce W. Wardropper |

| 1952–53 | *President:* | George Boas |
| | *Secretary:* | Earl Wasserman |

*Speakers * and Their Topics*

>>>>>>>>>>>>>>>>>>>>>>>>

1923

January 24, 1923   *George Boas*, A Phase of the History of Traditionalism from the Attempted Refutation of Condillac's Theory of the Origin of Language by Rousseau to the Condemnation of Bonetty by Pope Pius IX

March 1, 1923   *Gilbert Chinard*, Volney and Jefferson

April 26, 1923   *Arthur O. Lovejoy*, Some Current Errors about Rousseau

May 10, 1923   *A. Vermont*, Franklin and Some of his French Friends

1923–24

November 15, 1923   *C. C. Thach*, Montesquieu and the American Constitution.

December 13, 1923   *Jacob H. Hollander*, Discussion of the Ms. of J. S. Mill's *Autobiography*

---

* Except as noted otherwise, all lecturers were members of the Johns Hopkins University at the time of their addresses.

January 24, 1924   *Gustave L. Van Roosbroeck*, The Philosophic Background of Symbolism

February 20, 1924   *H. Carrington Lancaster*, Rationalistic Theories of the Origin of Language before the Eighteenth Century

March 20, 1924   *Marjorie Nicolson, Goucher College*, James Marsh and the Vermont Transcendentalists

April 17, 1924   *Gilbert Chinard*, Jefferson and France

1924–25

November 13, 1924   *Lois Whitney, Goucher College*, An Early Scotch Primitivist

December 17, 1924   *Adolph E. Zucker, University of Maryland*, The Genealogical Novel

January 22, 1925   *George Boas,* The Introduction of Kantianism into France

February 19, 1925   *Howard R. Patch, Smith College,* Chaucer and Lady Fortune

March 19, 1925   *Dumas Malone, University of Virginia,* Thomas Cooper and his Influence on his Time

April 16, 1925   *L. P. Shanks*, Flaubert's First Phase and the *Mal du Siècle*

1925–26

November 11, 1925   *Henry S. Jennings,* Some Adventures of the Evolution Idea at the Hands of the Biologists

December ? 1925	*Edward B. Mathews*, A History of Geological Thought
January 13, 1926	*Joseph S. Ames*, The History of the Concept of Light
February 8, 1926	*Jacob H. Hollander*, A Rediscovered MS. of Ricardo
March ? 1926	*W. W. Willoughby*, Political Pluralism and Guild Socialism
April 16, 1926	*E. A. Singer, Jr., University of Pennsylvania*, Death of the Western World, and Martyrdom of Man

1926–27

November 23, 1926	*Gilbert Chinard*, Nationalistic Primitivism in Eighteenth Century England
December 21, 1926	*Arthur O. Lovejoy*, The Meaning of Eighteenth Century Optimism
January 18, 1927	*William H. Welch*, The Erroneous Hypothesis and the Advancement of Knowledge
February 23, 1927	*George Boas*, French Theories of Internationalism in the Early Nineteenth Century
March 23, 1927	*Raymond D. Havens*, Thomas Warton and the Eighteenth Century Dilemma
April ? 1927	*Ford Brown, St. John's College*, Hannah More and the French Revolution

1927–28

November 11, 1927 — *Albert Feuillerat, University of Rennes,* Symposium: the Objectives of the Study of the History of Literature

December 15, 1927 — *Edwin Greenlaw,* A Sixteenth Century Battle of the Books

January 17, 1928 — *H. Carrington Lancaster,* Ideas about Politics, Marriage, Medicine, etc., in the French Drama of the Early Seventeenth Century

February 14, 1928 — *John C. Hemmeter, Baltimore,* Pre-requisites to a Philosophy of History

March 22, 1928 — *Gilbert Chinard,* Thomas Jefferson and the French Revolution

April 17, 1928 — *T. M. Raysor,* Coleridge's Rebuttal of Eighteenth Century Shakespearian Criticism

1928–29

November 22, 1928 — *Arthur O. Lovejoy,* Notes on Primitivism in Antiquity

December 20, 1928 — *Tenney Frank,* The Diffusion of Religions in the Roman Empire

January 10, 1929 — *Albert Schinz, University of Pennsylvania,* A New Approach to Rousseau

February 28, 1929 — *Edwin Greenlaw,* Notes towards a History of Research in the Seventeenth Century

| March 21, 1929 | *John R. Oliver*, Some Puzzles of the Hippocratean Corpus |
| May 2, 1929 | *George Boas*, Ideas about Animal Intelligence in the Sixteenth and Seventeenth Centuries |

1929-30

November 11, 1929	*Gilbert Chinard*, Thomas Jefferson: Philosopher of Americanism
December 12, 1929	*Hessell E. Yntema*, The Scientific Idea in Law
January 9, 1930	*Edward B. Mathews*, The Age of the Earth
February 13, 1930	*Adolf E. Zucker, University of Maryland,* The Ideas in Ibsen's Plays
March 12, 1930	*Stephen D'Irsay*, Public Opinion in the Medieval Universities
April 10, 1930	*W. Lee Ustick, Goucher College,* Some Seventeenth Century Books of Courtesy

1930-31

December 11, 1930	*George Boas*, Saturn and the Golden Age
January 15, 1931	*David Macht, Baltimore,* The Four Dimensions of Pharmacodynamics
January 30, 1931	*S. B. Liljegren, University of Greifswald,* Certain Aspects of Romanticism between Werther and Wilde
February 26, 1931	*Gilbert Chinard*, John Adams and the French Philosophers

March 12, 1931   *Kemp Malone,* Observations on Gilman's Hopkins

May 1, 1931   *Annette B. Hopkins, Goucher College,* Liberalism in the Social Teachings of Mrs. Gaskell

1931–32

November 18, 1931   *B. H. Hartogenesis,* Christian Domination of Maryland's Government Past and Present

December 15, 1931   *Hazelton Spencer,* The Metamorphosis of Prince Hamlet

January 20, 1932   *Arthur O. Lovejoy,* Grounds and Effects of the New Cosmography in the Seventeenth and Eighteenth Centuries

February 17, 1932   *W. Lee Ustick, Goucher College,* Changing Ideals of Aristocratic Character and Conduct in the Sixteenth and Seventeenth Centuries

March 16, 1932   *R. Florence Brinkley, Goucher College,* Political and Literary Use of the Arthurian Legend in the Seventeenth Century

April 27, 1932   *Kent Roberts Greenfield,* Some Currents of Thought on Social Questions in Northern Italy, 1815–1848

1932–33

November 16, 1932   *Buford Johnson,* Changing Conceptions in Individual Psychology

December 9, 1932	*Henry Sigerist,* Medical Theory and Medical Practice
January 25, 1933	*David Macht, Baltimore,* Alcohol, Nicotine and Coffee
February 15, 1933	*Irvin C. Holden,* The Present Status of Technocracy
March 23, 1933	*Louis I. Bredvold,* Pyrrhonism and Dryden's Catholicism

(Sixth meeting: minutes missing)

1933–34

(All minutes missing. Information from letters, diaries and other records)

November, 1933	No record
December 12, 1933	*Gordon Harper,* The Newman–Froude Letters
January 11, 1934	*Dorothy Stimson, Goucher College,* Comenius and the 'Invisible College'
February, 1934	*Harold Cherniss,* Aristotle's Criticism of the Pre-Socratics
March 8, 1934	*Paul E. Dumont,* Primitivism in Ancient India
April 12, 1934	*Ray Heffner,* The Defense of Constituted Authority by Spenser and Shakespeare

1934–35

(Minutes missing except for April. Information from other sources)

November, 1934	No record

December 13, 1934	*Sidney Painter*, The Ideas of Chivalry
January, 1935	No record
February 14, 1935	*W. Stull Holt*, The Idea of Scientific History in America
March 14, 1935	*Charles A. Beard*, " on the philosophy of history "
April 11, 1935	*Joseph S. Ames*, Fifty Years of American University Education
November or January ?	*Louis Teeter*, The Influence of Hobbes on Restoration Drama

1935–36

November 21, 1935	*Isaiah Bowman*, The Perils of the Adolescent Idea
December 12, 1935	*Raymond D. Havens*, Animism in Wordsworth
February 14, 1936	*Dorothy Miner, Walters Art Gallery*, The Idea of Artistic Originality in the Middle Ages
February 14, 1936	*Francis D. Murnaghan*, The Idea of Number
March 14, 1936	*H. Carrington Lancaster*, Louis XIV on the Stage
April 9, 1936	*Gustav Grünbaum*, Some Aspects of Humanism in Italy

1936–37

| November 12, 1936 | *George Boas*, A Note on the History of Taste |

December 10, 1936	*Ludwig Edelstein,* The Humanistic Approach to Greek and Roman Science
January 14, 1937	*Theodor Mommsen,* Early Tuscan Architecture in Terms of Spiritual and Political Science
February 27, 1937	*Niels Bohr, University of Copenhagen,* The Problem of Causality in Atomic Theory
April 1, 1937	*Carl Becker, Cornell University,* Some Limitations of Historical Evidence
April 8, 1937	*William F. Albright,* Art, Architecture and History

1937–38

November 18, 1937	*Leo Spitzer,* A Syntactic and Stylistic Feature of the Modern French Novel
December 8, 1937	*Francis D. Murnaghan,* The Basic Ideas of Arithmetic and Algebra
January 19, 1938	*Gilbert Chinard,* Planned Economy in the Eighteenth Century: Morelly's *Le Prince, La Basiliade* and *Code de la Nature*
February 10, 1938	*Kemp Malone,* Grundtvig's Philosophy of History
March 10, 1938	*J. von Neumann, Institute for Advanced Study, Princeton,* Causality and Modern Physics
April 14, 1938	*Eugene N. Curtis, Goucher College,* What was the French Revolution?

1938–39

November 17, 1938   *Arthur O. Lovejoy*, Some Prolegomena to a Possible History of Ideas concerning the Temporal Infinity of the World

December 15, 1938   *Hans Baren*, The Social Background of the Florentine Renaissance

January 12, 1939   *Owen Lattimore*, Central Asian Migrations and Conquests

February 9, 1939   *Albert K. Weinberg*, The Historical Meaning of the American Doctrine of Isolation

March 9, 1939   *Ola E. Winslow, Goucher College*, The Significance of Jonathan Edwards in American Religious History

April 14, 1939   *Johannes Mattern*, The Use and Abuse of Ideologies

1939–40

November 9, 1939   *Harold Cherniss*, The Biographical Fashion in Literary Criticism, with a reply read by *Townsend Scudder, Swarthmore College*

December 14, 1939   *Erwin Goodenough, Yale University*, Pictorial Symbol and Religious Idea in Classical Antiquity

January 11, 1940   *Sanford V. Larkey*, Magic and the Origin of Medicine

February 8, 1940	*Elio Gianturco, Library of Congress*, The Relation of the Thought of Montesquieu to that of Vico
March 14, 1940	*Arthur O. Lovejoy*, Notes on the Romantic Theory of Knowledge
April 18, 1940	*Lionello Venturi, New York City*, The Idea of Impressionism

1940–41

November 14, 1940	*F. Engel-Janosi*, Lord Acton's Ideas on History
December 12, 1940	*Arthur O. Lovejoy*, The Meaning of Romanticism for the Historian of Ideas
January 9, 1941	*Richard Shryock, University of Pennsylvania*, The Place of Method in the History of Social Thought
February 13, 1941	*Gerhardt H. Dieke*, The Development of New Ideas in Modern Physics
March 13, 1941	*John Shapley*, Virgil's Visible Immortality
April 10, 1941	*Leo Spitzer*, The Concept of Milieu and its History

1941–42

November 13, 1941	*George Boas*, A Basic Conflict in Aristotle's Philosophy
December 11, 1941	*Walter A. Patrick*, The Philosophy of Physical Science

January 8, 1942 *Gilbert Chinard, Princeton University,* Morelly Diderot, Rousseau and *Le Code de la Nature*

February 12, 1942 *Dorothy Stimson, Goucher College,* Some Reflections on Sprat's *History of the Royal Society*

March 12, 1942 *Samuel E. Morison, Harvard University,* The Stoic Background of General Washington

April 9, 1942 *Panos Morphopulos,* Guy de Brués and Sixteenth Century Scepticism in France

1942–43

November 12, 1942 *Francis R. Johnson, Stanford University,* Science and the Sixteenth Century Controversy over Improving the English Language

December 10, 1942 *Adolf Meyer,* The Concept of Ergasia

January 14, 1943 *F. Engel-Janosi, Catholic University,* Some Basic Ideas of the Historians of the Enlightenment

February 18, 1943 *Pedro Salinas,* The Defeat of 1898 and its Influence on Spanish Thought

March 11, 1943 *William F. Albright,* Historical Knowledge versus Scientific Knowledge

April 8, 1943 *Charles R. Anderson,* The Amateur Spirit in Ante-Bellum Charleston

1943–44

November 11, 1943 — *Ludwig Edelstein*, The Asclepius Cult and its Significance in Ancient Religion

December 9, 1943 — *Sidney Painter* and *Henry E. Sigerist* "read papers on Problems Facing the University"

January 13, 1944 — *Americo Castro, Princeton University*, The Ideological Foundations of Latin-American Culture

February 10, 1944 — *Carl B. Swisher*, The Commerce Clause of the Constitution: The History of its Interpretation

March 9, 1944 — *Scott Buchanan, St. John's College*, The Crisis of Liberal Education

April 13, 1944 — *Dorothy Miner, Walters Art Gallery*, The Transmittal of Artistic Ideas in Medieval Workshops

1944–45

November 9, 1944 — *George F. Carter*, Some Effects of the Idea of the Recency of Men in America

December 14, 1944 — *Rudolf Allers, Catholic University*, Psychology and Philosophy

January 11, 1944 — *Charles Singleton*, Dante's *Vita Nuova* and the Book of the Universe

February 8, 1945 — *Sidney Painter*, The Ideas of the Magna Carta

March 8, 1945   *Hajo Holborn, Yale University,* The Effect of Conscription on Modern European History

April 12, 1945   *Roy Pearce,* The Indian as Noble Savage: the American Concept, 1775-1810

1945-46

November 8, 1945 *Don C. Allen,* Some Seventeenth Century Notions of the Origination and Migration of Man

December 13, 1945 *Grace Frank, Bryn Mawr College,* The Impenitence of François Villon

January 10, 1946 *Jean Gottman,* Geographical Doctrines in Politics

February 14, 1946 *Richard E. Thursfield,* The Transmission of European Educational Ideas to the United States in the Nineteenth Century

March 14, 1946 *Wilson Shaffer,* The History of the Treatment of Mental Disease

April 11, 1946   *George Boas,* The Noble Savage in Medieval Thought and Legend

1946-47

November 14, 1946 *Arthur O. Lovejoy,* " Pride " in Seventeenth and Eighteenth Century Thought

December 12, 1946 *Joseph Blickensderfer, Library of Congress,* Lord Monboddo—Philosopher as Philologist

January 9, 1947	*Charles A. Barker*, Henry George's Idea of Social Justice
February 13, 1947	*Dorothy Stimson, Goucher College*, The Critical Years of the Royal Society, 1670–1703
March 13, 1947	*Donald H. Andrews*, Concepts of Freedom in Science and Philosophy
April 19, 1947	*Bentley Glass, Goucher College*, Maupertuis and the Beginnings of Genetics

1947–48

November 13, 1947	*Arthur O. Lovejoy* and *Don C. Allen*, two papers on China in the Eyes of Europe, 1580–1780
December 11, 1947	*René Wellek, Yale University*, Six Types of Literary History
January 8, 1948	*Owsei Temkin*, Medicine and the Problem of Moral Responsibility
February 12, 1948	*Helen Dodson, University of Michigan*, Changing Conceptions of the Sun
March 11, 1948	*William L. Straus*, Theories of Human Origin
April 8, 1948	*Erich Auerbach, Pennsylvania State College*, An Historical Explanation of Nineteenth Century Realism

1948–49

November 11, 1948   *Harold Cherniss, Institute for Advanced Study, Princeton University*, The History of Ideas and Ancient Greek Philosophy

December 10, 1948   *Basil Willey, Cambridge University*, George Eliot

January 13, 1949   *Elizabeth Nitchie, Goucher College*, Longinus and English Literary Criticism

February 10, 1949   *Leslie Peck*, Number and Infinity

March 10, 1949   *Victor Lowe*, Source-Hunting in Philosophy and its Application to the Philosophy of Whitehead

April 14, 1949   *Fritz Machlup*, The Idea of Private Property in Ideas

1949–50

November 9, 1949   *William F. Albright*, Biblical Criticism in the Light of the New Scrolls: A Test of the Literary-Historical Method

December 7, 1949   *Thomas I. Cook*, The Idea of Democracy

January 12, 1950   *Conway Zirkle, University of Pennsylvania*, The History of the Idea of "Pangenesis"

February 9, 1950   *Otto F. Kraushaar, Goucher College*, Evolution and Ethics

March 10, 1950	*Peter Viereck, Mount Holyoke College,* Prince Chaadayev and his *Lettres Philosophiques*: Russia's Literary and Political Catalyst
April 13, 1950	*George Boas,* The Arts and the *Encyclopédie*

1950–51

November 9, 1950	*Owen Lattimore,* The Origin and Recent Development of Revolutionary Ideas in China
December 14, 1950	*Raymond D. Havens,* Simplicity, a Changing Concept
January 11, 1951	*Richard H. Shryock,* Changing Concepts of the Nature of Disease
February 15, 1951	*Elio Gianturco, Washington, D. C.,* Vico and the Social Sciences
March 8, 1951	*Carol K. Bang,* Polarity in Strindberg's Conception of Women
April 12, 1951	*Graham Hough, University of Cambridge,* The Influence of Coleridge's Ideas on the Victorian Age

1951–52

November 8, 1951	*Ludwig Edelstein,* Plato's Political Theory
December 6, 1951	*Earl R. Wasserman,* The Divine Analogy in the Eighteenth Century

Speakers and Their Topics

January 10, 1952	*Alexandre Koyré, École des Hautes Études, Paris,* Metaphysical Factors in the Evolution of Science
February 14, 1952	*Eric Vogelin, Louisiana State University,* The Discovery of the Soul—in Ancient and Modern Philosophy
March 13, 1952	*Robert T. Clark, University of Texas,* Wieland and the Combinatory System
May 1, 1952	*T. S. Ashton, London School of Economics,* The Treatment of Capitalism by Historians

Index

Index

Index

I

Iamblichus: 49, 63, 65
Ibsen: 204
Idea, meaning of in history of ideas: 3; and semasiology, 4
Idealism in America: 168
Ideas: ancient Greek history of, 215; efficacy and aetiology of, 15
Ideologies: 209
Iltis: 149
Impersonal verbs: 85
Impressionism: 210
Infection: history of concept of, article on, 123; definition of, 123; derivation of word, 124; and contagion, 135; secularization of concept of, 144; summary history of idea of, 145
Infinity: temporal of the world, 209; and number, 215
Internationalism: 202
Isolation, American doctrine of: 209
Italy: social question in, 205; humanism in, 207

J

James, Henry: 10, 161
James, William: 166
Jefferson: 96, 102, 120, 200–204
Jennings, Henry S.: 201
Johns Hopkins University, problems facing: 212
Johnson, Buford: 205
Johnson, Francis R.: 211
Journal of the History of Ideas: 169, 191
Julian: 49

K

Kant: 107, 167, 201
Knowledge: anomaly of, 18; advancement of, 202; romantic theory of, 210
Koch: 123, 145
Kölreuter: 153
Koyré, Alexander: 217
Kraushaar, Otto F.: 215

L

Lancaster, H. C.: 178, 185, 190, 197–99, 201, 203, 207
Lane, Fred: 198
Language: article on, 67; and convention, 69; refinements on, 69; and ambiguity, 70; and the community, 72; historians of, 77; kinships of various, 77; universal features of, 79; metaphysical and religious import of, 86; and poetry, 87; origin of, 200–201
Larkey, Sanford P.: 198, 209
Latin-American culture: 212
Lattimore, Owen: 209, 216
Law: 204
Leibniz: 11
Leprosy: 125
Leucippus: 32
Leviticus: 125
Lichtenberg: 69, 84, 86
Liebig: 137
Light: 202
Liljegren, S. B.: 204
Linguistics, apologia of: 83
Linnaeus: 153
Lister: 123, 145
Literary criticism: 209
Literary history: 203, 214
Littré: 134
Locke: 107
Logos: 24, 25
Longinus: 88, 215
Louis XIV: 207
Lovejoy, A. O.: 4, 5, 13, 18, 21, 47, 48, 66, 94, 163, 175, 197, 198, 200, 202, 203, 205, 209, 210, 213, 214; rôle in American philosophy, article on, 161
Lowe, Victor: 180, 199, 215
Lucian: 55
Lucretius: 8, 88, 93

M

Machlup, Fritz: 199, 215
Macht, David: 204, 206
Macrobius: 48, 66
Madison, Bishop: 120
Magic: 209
Magna Carta: 212
Malakis, Emile: 198
Malebranche: 107
Malone, Dumas: 201
Malone, Kemp: 177, 180, 181, 197, 198, 205, 208
Malthus, in Miller: 114
Man: origination and migration, 213; recency in America, 212
Marsh, James: 201
Marxism, and history of ideas: 13

Index

Index